Daniel B Donald

D0622412

THE EFFECTIVE MINISTER

The Effective Minister

Psychological and Social Considerations

Michael E. Cavanagh

1817

Harper & Row, Publishers, San Francisco

Cambridge, Hagerstown, New York, Philadelphia, Washington
London, Mexico City, São Paulo, Singapore, Sydney

Acknowledgment is made to the following for permission to reprint copyrighted material: *The Jerusalem Bible*, copyright © 1966 by Darton, Longman & Todd, Inc., and Doubleday and Company, Inc. Used by permission. *The Reality of Jesus* by Dermot A. Lane copyright © 1975 by Dermot A. Lane; used by permission of Paulist Press. *The Roots of Unbelief* by William J. O'Malley; copyright © 1976 by the Missionary Society of St. Paul the Apostle in the State of New York; used by permission of Paulist Press. *Your Pastor's Problems* by William E. Hulme, copyright © 1977 by Augsburg Publishing House; reprinted by permission. *The Book of Sacramental Basics* by Tad Guzie; copyright © 1981 by Tad Guzie; used by permission of Paulist Press.

THE EFFECTIVE MINISTER. Copyright © 1986 by Michael E. Cavanagh. All rights reserved. Printed in the United States of America. No part of this book may be used or reproduced in any manner whatsoever without written permission except in the case of brief quotations embodied in critical articles and reviews. For information address Harper & Row, Publishers, Inc., 10 East 53rd Street, New York, NY 10022. Published simultaneously in Canada by Fitzhenry & Whiteside, Limited, Toronto.

FIRST EDITION

Library of Congress Cataloging-in-Publication Data

Cavanagh, Michael E.
   The effective minister.

   Bibliography: p. 205.
   1. Clergy—Office. 2. Pastoral theology. 3. Lay ministry. I. Title.
BV660.2.C38   1986   253   86–51006
ISBN 0-06-254210-9

86 87 88 89 90 RRD 10 9 8 7 6 5 4 3 2 1

Contents

Introduction

This book is written for all Christian ministers, male or female, nonordained or ordained, who, on a full- or part-time basis, attempt to introduce people to Jesus Christ, his teachings, values, and love. In the past few years, the concept of ministry has broadened to include not only ordained ministers, but also the nonordained who are baptized followers of Jesus Christ and who publicly teach, counsel, and celebrate according to his teachings.

From the Roman Catholic perspective, an example of this concept is found in a tract entitled *As One Who Serves*, prepared for the (Roman Catholic) Bishops' Committee on Priestly Life:

The service of ministry *(diakonia)* has a corporate character. For all those made one by Baptism into Christ thereby share in his ministry. Ministry, then, is the vocation, privilege and responsibility of all members of the Church.[1]

From a Protestant perspective, Oscar Feucht writes in his book, *Everyone a Minister*:

No less than six titles are given to the Christian in 1 Peter 2:5,9. They are based on Old Testament promises and figures of speech. According to this catalog of titles every Christian is claimed by God, belongs to a holy nation, is set apart for a particular ministry, has both a "kingship" and a "priesthood" of his own to fulfill in his life. It is significant that these are the words of the apostle Peter, one of the three disciples closest to our Lord. These titles raise all believers to the status of "ministers."[2]

My purpose in writing this book is to share some ideas, perspectives, criticisms, and hopes that may be helpful to ministers in their efforts to grow as human beings, Christians, and ministers. I have tried to write this book in a style that is unvarnished, honest, realistic, and stratified so that it can be equally meaningful to ministers with great experience and to those who are just beginning their ministry.

My interest in writing the book stems from several sources:

- My five years in a seminary, which gave me some appreciation of the nature, the rigors, and the rewards of ministry;

- My experiences as a Christian who has had at least his share of dealings with ministers, as a parishioner, and as a student from early childhood to the present;

- My experiences as a clinical psychologist who has worked with many ministers over the past twenty years in both educational and counseling situations;

- My experience as a minister to ministers, which has given me a hands-on feeling for the joys and sorrows, hopes and discouragements, successes and failures, peace and anxiety, faith and despair that are a part of being a Christian minister.

This book is written for all Christian ministers because pastoral needs, competencies, values, problems, and goals span all denominations. However, a few issues discussed in the book, such as sexuality, may be more pertinent to Roman Catholic ministry.

As is true with any book on ministry, this one can treat only a relatively small sample of topics. The topics were chosen on the bases that they are the issues ministers have most asked me to address in lectures and workshops, and the issues in which I have a particular interest or have had the most experience.

This book was not written to be read at one, two, or three sittings. I have tried to include a good deal of thought- and emotion-provoking material on each page. Thus, it is a book to meditate upon. My hope is that each minister will bring at least one thought, feeling, and resolution away from the book that will make his or her life and ministry more fulfilling and effective.

1. The Psychologically and Pastorally Effective Minister

A violin is a musical instrument that is both sensitive and strong. It is sensitive in that it is affected by the slightest touch, and it is strong because its strings can withstand a good deal of pressure. A violin must be continually and properly tuned to be played well, for it if is not, even the finest violinist cannot call forth beautiful music from it.

As an instrument of the Lord, a minister shares these qualities with a violin. Ministers must be sensitive enough to feel with people yet strong enough to withstand pressure. When ministers are in tune with themselves, they can touch people in beautiful ways, but when they are out of tune with themselves, not even the Lord can make music with them.

There is one area in which the above analogy does not hold. While someone must continually tune the violin, the minister alone is responsible for keeping himself or herself in tune.

No one expects a minister to be perfectly sensitive, strong, and in tune, but everyone expects a minister to function at least adequately, if not well, in most situations. To do this requires more than good intentions and hard work. *As One Who Serves* states the matter clearly and succinctly.

A person who is a servant leader is expected to be a healthy, maturing person . . . . In reality, the dimensions or responsibilities of [the minister] as servant leader are realizable only in the context of the [minister] as a person. Such development includes the emotional, intellectual, and spiritual dimensions of growth.[1]

It is toward this end that the present chapter is written. The first part of the chapter deals with some of the aspects of being a psychologically healthy minister; the second part discusses some of the qualities of a pastorally effective minister. The concepts in this chapter are targets to shoot for, goals on which to focus. No minister fully possesses all the qualities that will be discussed, but all ministers should possess them to a greater, rather than a lesser, degree if they realistically expect to be effective instruments of the Lord.

ASPECTS OF A HEALTHY SENSE OF SELF

The "self" has rarely enjoyed a positive place in Christianity. In its appropriate concern with the sins of selfishness and self-indulgence, the Church overshot the mark and enjoined Christians to become "selfless." Thus the self has often been viewed as a significant obstacle to charity, spirituality, and eternal happiness. Selfless people denied and abrogated their selves to "higher" pursuits. In fact, during one period in Church history, people—many of whom were later to be canonized—publicly vied with each other to see who could best humble his or her self.

Although the concerns of the Church were valid, they tended to cause the Church to throw out the baby with the bath. We now realize that a selfless person is no more apt to be a good Christian than is a selfish one. As with most human behaviors, virtue lies in moderation.

From a personal standpoint, to ignore or disparage the self is to treat poorly a beautiful gift from God. It is far more appropriate to nourish, protect, and celebrate the self than it is to torture it or allow it to die through neglect. From an interpersonal point of view, ignoring the self is analogous to an ambulance driver ignoring and mistreating the engine of his ambulance, even though he does so because he is busy transporting people to the hospital. Sooner or later, the ambulance is likely to run out of gas or fail mechanically and threaten the safety of the very people the driver is trying to help. No one would view an ambulance driver who takes good care of his ambulance as selfish; nor would it be proper to view a minister who takes good psychological care of his or her self as selfish.

Like all Christians and all human beings, ministers have not only the right but the responsibility to celebrate their selves and to take proper care of them, both for their own welfare and the welfare of others. It is virtually impossible for a minister who attends properly to his or her self to experience burnout or other psychological problems. This type of thinking is not new, nor do its roots lie in humanism, personalism, modernism, or psychogism. One need only look to Jesus and the healthier of the saints to see that there is good precedent for proper attention to the self.

SELF-KNOWLEDGE

"Know thyself," said Socrates. The possession of self-knowledge is the first aspect of a healthy sense of self. The self is analogous to a terrain that is smooth in parts, rough in others, and also marbled with gullies and dead-end roads. A minister who has an accurate self-map will arrive at his or her destination with a minimum amount of difficulty. If clouds of defense mechanisms cover parts of the terrain, a minister will experience inordinate difficulties, and may fall, get lost, or arrive at a dead end.

Because both ministers and their environments are changing each minute and each day, self-knowledge is transitory and always incomplete. However, the more self-knowledge ministers acquire, the more appropriate, constructive, and expeditious their behavior will be. The more inaccurate the map, the more inappropriate, destructive, and wasteful their behavior will be.

The following four dimensions of the self are particularly relevant to a minister's effective functioning: one's strengths, weaknesses, motives for acting, and social behavior or impressions.

It is important to recognize one's strong points and to use them to the advantage of oneself and others. Some ministers are unaware of their strengths, and, like a carpenter who is unaware of the tools available, such ministers unnecessarily function at less than optimal levels.

Maybe one of a minister's strengths is the presence of a clear view of reality which can see through tangential issues to the heart of a problem or a situation. Perhaps a minister is capable of great empathy and relates easily with people who are experiencing hurts, fears, angers, or guilts. A minister may have a sound spirituality that enables him or her to place events in a spiritual perspective and to share this perspective in a way that encourages and heals others.

Effective ministers do not mechanically use their strengths as a surgeon uses surgical instruments. But they are aware of their strengths and do not hesitate to capitalize on them when they are most needed or when nothing else seems to be helpful at a particular time.   *Anger ; impatience*

Besides being aware of their strengths, ministers do well to pay attention to their weaknesses. Ministers who are oblivious to their weaknesses will make the same mistakes over and over again, damaging themselves and others in the process. A minister may tend to be impatient and sometimes treat people as intruders. Instead of asking, "What can *I* do for you?" such a minister asks, "What do *you* want?" Sometimes a minister may tend to use and manipulate people, employing the justification that it is for their own good, when it is actually for the minister's good. Maybe a minister unintentionally harbors biases toward members of the same sex or the opposite sex, toward certain races, classes of people, or religious denominations, or toward certain problems.

Ministers who are unaware of these weaknesses become blunted instruments of the Lord. If they can admit their weaknesses to themselves and to others, they have a good chance to control them, work on them, and ultimately reduce them or even turn them into strengths.

If ministers want to grow in self-knowledge, they have to recognize the motives behind their actions. It is not unusual for people to be unaware of their reasons for making certain decisions or for behaving in certain ways. As human beings, we typically are aware of motives that cause us to feel good about ourselves and unaware of those that create anxiety. When we are aware of some of our motives but unaware of others, we become virtually two people, one of whom is a stranger to the other. This can cause significant confusion and damage to ourselves and others.

For example, a minister chooses to work in an inner-city parish. The minister's choice may be based on the conscious motivation that the poor and oppressed need her more than do middle-class or wealthy people. However, the minister's unconscious motivation is that she expects to receive more appreciation from the inner-city people and be viewed by others as dedicated and strong. When, after a short time, it becomes clear to her that she is actually receiving less appreciation than she did from other people and that people view her no differently than they did before—or perhaps that they view her as foolish—the minister's motivation weakens considerably. Soon she experiences frustration and discouragement and blames her reactions on an unchangeable social system. This allows her to leave the inner-city ministry without ever coming to grips with her deeper motives. Even though the minister blames others for the situation, abandoning this ministry is not good for her: it leaves her experiencing a sense of failure. Nor is the leaving good for the people: the minister was just beginning to develop a reputation as someone who genuinely cared about them, and when she left, the people perceived her as deserting them.

Commonly, hidden motives deal with the needs to acquire power, prestige, attention, romance, control, and the needs to be perceived as competent, holy, intelligent, attractive, clever, successful. None of these motives is inherently problematic; they become so only when they are disguised by other motives that appear more acceptable to the person and others.

It is important for ministers to be aware of their social behavior, that is, the impressions that they are giving people. Unfortunately, the impressions we give are not always what we think they are or would like them to be. For example, a minister thinks he gives the impression of being concerned and friendly as he greets people after services. But his ingenuine smile and his superficial and overplayed attempts to be friendly give the impression of a politician trying to win votes from people about whom he could not care less. So, while his fantasy is that people are admiring his friendliness, they are actually commenting on his phoniness.

Another minister believes that she is impressing people with her knowledge of psychology and theology. Her pedantic style, name-dropping, and unnecesasry use of abstract terms actually leave the impression that she is insecure and intellectually narcissistic.

Ministers should give good impressions, but the good impressions should flow spontaneously from their goodness and not be manufactured by the need to be different than they really are. When ministers receive feedback that the impressions they are giving people are unhelpful, they can attempt to discover who they are trying to be that they are not, and they can seek a constructive resolution to the discrepancy.

II. SELF-ESTEEM

The second aspect of a healthy sense of self is self-esteem. Self-esteem does not mean pride or narcissism. It simply means that ministers with self-esteem treat themselves as they treat others whom they esteem, that is, with kindness and respect. They also expect to be treated in helpful ways, or at least in ways that do not unduly impair their effectiveness, freedom, or happiness. Ministers who possess at least adequate self-esteem share the following qualities: they have self-respect; they like themselves; they stand up for themselves; and they treat themselves well.

The first quality flowing from self-esteem is self-respect. Self-respect, in turn, helps ministers to communicate clearly who they are without equivocating on their beliefs, feelings, or values. Self-respecting ministers are themselves at all times, and except for superficial differences, they are not more themselves in one situation and less themselves in another. They do not overidentify with the role of minister, wearing it like a cloak to hide their insecurities, inadequacies, ignorance, or doubts. They operate on the principle, "This is who I am right now. I hope you like it, but if you don't, I'd rather be disliked for who I am than liked for who I'm not."

Ministers who lack self-esteem do not respect and/or like who they are, either because they distort their goodness through a negative lens of unrealistic expectations and false beliefs, or because they behave in ways that do not merit respect and esteem. These ministers represent themselves in ways that are unclear, confusing, and contradictory because they need to hide behind smokescreens. They are chameleonlike, changing colors with the psychological and theological terrain. They are one person in the presence of an authority, a second in the presence of friends, a third with family, a fourth with their congregation, a fifth with other ministers, and a sixth when they are alone. They are influenced by powerful and dramatic people, whose mannerisms and values they assume, forsaking their own selves in the process.

Besides possessing self-respect, ministers with self-esteem like themselves. This leads them to appreciate being who they are, to enjoy spending time with themselves, and to enjoy sharing themselves with others.

Ministers who lack adequate self-esteem are basically dissatisfied with themselves and, deep down, wish they were someone else, someone more attractive, intelligent, admired, popular, powerful, or successful. They continually strive after these qualities and/or pretend to themselves and others that they possess them. This causes a continuing state of unrest, the reverberations of which affect the people around them.

Ministers who lack adequate self-esteem seldom enjoy being by themselves. They need to be preoccupied with people and projects so that they do not have to spend time with someone they dislike and find boring, namely, themselves.

Ministers who lack adequate self-esteem are reluctant to share themselves with people because they fear that others will see them as they see themselves and reject them, as they have rejected themselves. As a result, they remain psychologically distant from others, or they place a transparent shield around their hearts, leading people to believe that they are approachable when, in fact, sooner or later it will become obvious that they are not.

Ministers with self-esteem possess a third important quality:

they stand up for themselves. They do not allow others to treat them unjustly, to unduly restrict their freedom, or to manipulate them into behaving in ways that are inconsistent with who they are. They see to it that they get what they deserve and that they are allowed to exercise a reasonable degree of free choice. They do not allow themselves to be pressured into behaviors, relationships, or situations that are inimical to their psychological and spiritual well-being.

Ministers who lack self-esteem allow themselves to be ignored and passed over, or to be overburdened when it is inappropriate and destructive. They allow themselves to be imprisoned by the inordinate needs and expectations of others and to be intimidated into behaviors, decisions, and projects for which they are unmotivated and ill-suited. As a result, they feel even lower self-esteem, which creates an endless vicious cycle.

Finally, ministers with self-esteem treat themselves well. This means that they care for themselves as they would care for anyone they like and respect. Their work schedule is reasonable; that is, they do not overwork and sap their energy, effectiveness, and joy; nor do they underwork and feel lethargic, bored, or purposeless. They assiduously avoid relationships and situations that are inordinately depleting and damaging. When it becomes clear that they are in a relationship or a situation in which they are being treated as a scapegoat, a slave, a punching bag, a martyr, a bodyguard, a baby-sitter, or a referee, they disengage themselves, regardless of what others think about them. They have no need to be a victim of anyone or anything.

Such ministers allow themselves adequate leisure time so that they can relax, introspect, enjoy, and rejuvenate themselves. Leisure-time is given a high priority, and it is not viewed as something tagged on to the end of the day or the week if there is no other work to do. They confine the majority of their energies, thoughts, and feelings to the present, refusing to mourn the past or fret over the future. Each day is an amorphous piece of clay that they can sculpt to the best advantage of themselves and others.

Ministers with self-esteem keep their emotional slate clear. Each significant emotion is acknowledged and expressed spontaneously and appropriately. As a result, by the end of the workday, they are sufficiently buoyant and can enjoy the second half of their day. Ministers with less self-esteem hesitate to express their feelings for fear of losing what limited self-esteem they have. They bottle up their feelings of hurt, anger, fear, and frustration, which adds excess weight to their psyche, body, and soul. They collapse at the end of the workday, rueing all the opportunities they had to change things simply by expressing their feelings. They tell anyone who will listen what they *should* have said, what they *could* have done, what they *felt like* saying. Their unexpressed feelings curdle within them and turn sour, causing them to begin each new day with a larger handicap.

Ministers with self-esteem treat themselves well by making decisions based on the best information available, realizing that a certain percentage of their decisions will turn out less well than they hoped. After they make the decision, they leave it and move on to the next challenge. They do not torture themselves (and others) with indecision, confusion, needless worry, second-guessing, and rumination.

They walk into relationships and situations with their heads up, choosing how they will get involved and for how long. They do not allow themselves to get caught in the wake of other people's needs, getting swept into situations by currents that were too subtle for them to see or too powerful for them to resist. They rarely find themselves lamenting, "How did I get myself into this mess?" or "I knew this wasn't a good idea."

Ministers with self-esteem possess a healthy sense of self-discipline, which frees them to function well. They structure their day and use it well. They do not have long periods of useless time; nor do they overschedule their day, having to leave appointments early only to get to the next appointment late. They eat, drink, and sleep in moderation, refusing to punish their bodies with excess weight or substances that damage tissues or impair thinking. They get an adequate amount of exercise and keep in reasonably good shape so that their bodies will continue to be strong encasements for their psyches and souls.

III SELF-ACTUALIZATION

The third aspect of the healthy self is the ability for self-actualization. This means that effective ministers are self-motivated, self-directing, self-confident, and self-sustaining.

Self-motivating means that ministers must possess intrinsic motivation; that is, they must be self-starters. They must know what they have to do on any particular day, and then do it. Intrinsic motivation is the opposite of both extrinsic motivation and no motivation. Extrinsic motivation means that a minister does not make any significant decisions or take any meaningful action until pressured by others to do so. This causes frustration in other people and resentment in the minister. No motivation means that a minister's laziness, insecurities, fears, frustrations, and resentments have short-circuited his or her motivation, leaving him or her immobilized. This creates dullness or helplessness in the minister and frustration and withdrawal in other people.

The self-actualized minister is also self-directing. This means that psychologically healthy ministers basically make and carry out their own decisions. They examine each important situation with reasonable care, scrutinize the relevant issues, consult with others, make their decision, and accept the responsibility for the consequences.

Therefore, self-actualized and self-directing ministers must also possess reasonable self-confidence; that is, confidence in their intuitions, perceptions, judgments, and decisions. This enables ministers to assert themselves, sharing their ideas, feelings, and values in a clear and forthright manner. Self-confidence does not mean that ministers are confident that they are always correct. It simply means that they are confident that what they say is generally worth considering and will help clarify situations. Such ministers recognize that they will not always be on target, but they are willing at least to illuminate the target with their input.

There are two ways in which ministers can experience difficulty with self-confidence. The first is to believe that they are always, or almost always, correct. Paradoxically, this belief indicates a lack of self-confidence, which, in turn, prevents ministers from seeing their imperfections and taking appropriate corrective action. The second difficulty is that these ministers may not move or progress until they possess absolute moral certitude. Since they rarely, if ever, feel so certain, they remain reticent on anything but the most superficial issues. Both difficulties have the same negative side effects: they render ministers useless as catalysts who could create illumination; and they prevent ministers from being sought after by people who need someone off whom to deflect concerns.

Finally, self-actualized ministers are self-sustaining. This means that ministers must sustain themselves without overrelying on others for their survival. Ministers need to be capable of meeting their own needs for security, freedom, success, justice, stimulation, and leisure.

With regard to interpersonal needs, self-actualized ministers see to it that they relate to people socially (in contrast to pastorally) who are able and willing to participate in mutually fulfilling relationships; that is, to those who are willing to give and receive affection, to trust and be trusted, to give freedom and accept it, to give joy and accept it, to give honesty and receive it.

Sometimes ministers confuse being self-sustaining with being self-sufficient; that is, needing no one else for growth and happiness. This confusion can lead ministers into three problem areas. The first problem is that they may live a half life by depriving themselves of the growth and the joy of getting interpersonal needs met. As a result, these ministers go through life functioning on only half of their psychological and theological cylinders, and they are often unaware of their retardation.

A second problem is that these ministers may experience a deep-seated loneliness, the pain of which they may try to anesthetize with work, prayer, avocations, food, drink, sex, or drugs. However, neither the pain nor its source is ever completely excised, and thus never really dealt with.

A third problem with confusing self-sustenance with self-suffi-
ciency is that seemingly self-sufficient ministers might convey
the message that they need no one. This causes people to be disinterested in them and remain distant, which, in turn, impairs
the minister's apostolic functions.

Some ministers may lack self-sustenance altogether. They may
be unwilling or incapable of foraging for themselves; hence they
are almost totally reliant on others for nourishment. This dependency places them in a perilously vulnerable position: when they
please others, they get fed, but when they displease others, they
starve. In order to survive, these ministers must cater to the
needs, values, and whims of others, even at the sacrifice of their
overall well-being. These ministers are like people who voluntar-
ily hand over their lives to gain simple food and shelter.

IV. SELF-FULFILLMENT

The fourth aspect of a healthy sense of self is self-fulfillment. Just
as ministers have physical appetites, they also have psychological appetites. The more psychosocial needs they get met, the
more they grow in psychological strength. When ministers fail to
get their needs met adequately, three conditions can result: psychological malnutrition, psychological semistarvation, and psychological starvation.

Psychological malnutrition results when a minister is getting
some needs met, but not enough to remain healthy. Some common symptoms of psychological anemia are inordinate discouragement, irritability, confusion, indecision, frustration, hurt,
resentment, guilt, cynicism, jealousy, forgetfulness, procrastina-
tion, or distractability.

Psychological semistarvation results when a minister is getting
no important needs met to any meaningful degree. Some typical
semistarvation symptoms are clinical depression, anxiety reactions, phobias, obsessions, compulsions, alcoholism, depersonal-
ization, drug abuse, sexual disorders, or psychophysiological reactions (tension headaches, peptic ulcers, compulsive eating,
frequent colds, insomnia, high blood pressure, psychogenic men-
strual disorders, etc.).

Psychological starvation results from a minister not getting important needs met over a prolonged period of time. Some common starvation symptoms are acute disorientation, serious mood disorders (manic and depressive disorders), schizophrenic disorders, and paranoid reactions.

Most, if not all, ministers require the following "self" needs to be fulfilled in order to minister effectively.

Like other people, ministers need affection. They need to have one or more people need, appreciate, affirm, trust, and support them. They need to have people pay attention to them, demonstrate warmth, tenderness, and empathy, perceive them as special, and love them.

Ministers also need to give affection. This is an underrated need, but one that is as important as receiving affection. It consists of behaving in ways that allow one or more people to feel loved, understood, appreciated, treasured, special, secure, worthwhile, joyful, free to be themselves, and loved.

Ministers need to exercise freedom. Although ministers realize that reality imposes some unavoidable restrictions, ministers remain unfulfilled—and thus unhealthy—unless they are allowed freedoms such as the following: to pick their friends; to decide the direction of their important decisions; to judge when they will or will not make sacrifices; to determine what their life-style will or will not be; to select what professional and religious values they will espouse or eschew; to resolve how long they will stay in a relationship or a situation and when they will leave it; and to choose to whom they do or do not owe loyalty.

The healthy minister needs to experience stimulation. Although a certain amount of routine is inevitable in life, ministers must see to it that they have a sufficient degree of variety, change, newness, and freshness in their lives. Thus, they should refuse to be stifled by avoidable routine in their jobs, relationships, or life in general.

Ministers need to feel a sense of accomplishment. While healthy ministers understand that they cannot always see all the fruits of their labors, they make sure that they are able to see some positive results and tangible rewards of their efforts and endeavors in their occupations or personal lives. This helps ministers feel that who they are and what they are doing are worthwhile.

Ministers need solitude. Privacy and peace and quiet enable ministers to remain in touch with themselves, to relax, think, pray, or just quietly be.

Ministers need to be treated justly. While ministers should realize that they are not immune to injustice, they also need to be afforded the respect, freedom, support, recognition, and rewards that they deserve in important relationships and situations.

Ministers need to have hope. They need to see a light at the end of the tunnel. At some perceivable point in the future, ministers must have the hope to experience a reasonable degree of success or relief from distress.

Healthy ministers need a purpose in their lives. Ministers need a value, a philosophy, or a theology that ties their days, endeavors, joys, and sufferings into one meaningful theme that serves as a frame of reference, a source of encouragement, and an ultimate goal.

Finally, ministers need joy for self-fulfillment. While healthy ministers realize that life is often difficult and sometimes almost impossible, they also see to it that they experience a reasonable amount of joy. They experience joy from a variety of areas and enterprises: doing a good job, reading, writing, relaxing, athletics, music, art, nature, exercise, social activities, looking attractive, prayer, and relationships.

These "self" (psychosocial) needs are common in our culture and probably in all modern cultures. They seem to stem from a combination of biological predisposition and learning. These needs differ in intensity from one person to another, and even within the same person at different times, much the same as do physical needs. Like anyone else, ministers can go about getting these needs met consciously or unconsciously. A minister may consciously decide he needs some joy in his life, so he takes the day off to play tennis, walk along the seashore, or visit a dear friend. Or, without consciously knowing why, a minister may decide it is time to disengage herself from a relationship or a job that has been subtly and gradually usurping her freedom. Both decisions—conscious and unconscious—fulfill the minister's need for joy in life.

Unfortunately, because deprivation in psychosocial needs does not register the clear warning signals that physical need deprivation does, ministers can go for prolonged periods of time depriving themselves of fulfillment in one or more critical areas. The same minister who would never miss a meal or a night's sleep may go for months or even years without getting his need for affection, freedom, stimulation, or joy adequately met. All the while he wonders why he is suffering the psychological hunger pains of fatigue, irritability, illness, anxiety, forgetfulness, depression, cynicism, hopelessness, or spiritual desolation.

It is also important to realize that simply because a minister is in a situation where she "should" be getting her needs met, it does not necessarily mean that they are being met. The minister may have a family or live with a religious community, but the people in her life may not be willing to meet or capable of meeting many of her needs with any degree of consistency. Even if they may be willing to meet and capable of meeting her needs, her unresolved fears, resentments, or guilts may keep her from accepting their love, freedom, or joy.

It is necessary for ministers to understand what their specific needs are, how important each is at any given time, and how he or she plans on getting them met with reasonable consistency. Just as ministers need to eat and sleep each day, they need to get at least some of their needs met each day. It is not sufficient to set aside two weeks a year to relax or four days a year to experience joy.

It is important that ministers see to it that they get their needs met; that is, that they do not wait passively to be fed by others. Psychologically vibrant ministers arrange their time, work, relationships, and prayer so that most days are at least reasonably, if not maximally, fulfilling. Ministers who suffer from psychological malnutrition typically protest that, due to the way their life is

Passive arranged, they cannot possibly get their needs met adequately. These same ministers would never allow others to arrange their days so that they did not eat or sleep. Sometimes it takes professional help—and in some cases a great deal of help—to get a minister to the point where he or she will assume personal responsibility for his or her psychological diet and nourishment.

Unfortunately, like anyone else, ministers may be unaware of crucial needs within themselves, either because the need has never been primed or because the minister has repressed the need. A minister who has seldom or never experienced true love may be unaware of his need for love. This need may lie dormant throughout life, or become primed only later in life. Again, a minister may repress the need for love because she realizes, at least subconsciously, that if she allows it to surface, it will create great anxiety. On some level the minister knows that if it surfaces but is not met, she will experience great loneliness, which she does not wish to do. If she attempts to reach out to people for love, she may become overdependent on someone, and thus lose her freedom, or she may be rejected. Unconsciously, the minister has decided to let sleeping dogs lie.

Finally, it is important that ministers do not perceive the concept of need fulfillment as selfish or self-indulgent, any more than they view eating three meals a day or sleeping eight hours a night as selfish or self-indulgent. Ministers who do not see to it that their psychosocial needs are met reasonably well each day will be of no better use to themselves or others than if they were to skip a meal or two each day. To the extent that ministers are not psychosocially fulfilled, they cannot be spiritually healthy, nor can they adequately fulfill the psychosocial and spiritual needs of others. Ministers cannot give what they do not have.

In summary, the self of the minister is basic to who he or she is. It is the minister's motor, steering mechanism, and brake. A healthy self provides the minister with good energy, with good steering that allows the minister to stay on the road, and with good brakes for slowing down and stopping when it is appropriate. A less healthy self gives the minister too much or too little energy, poor steering (making it difficult to stay on the road), and defective brakes (causing the minister to slow down and stop when he or she should not or fail to stop when he or she should).

Like an automobile, the self requires continual maintenance. The effects of poor maintenance on the self are the same as on an automobile: sooner or later the minister sputters to a stop, blows up, crashes into something, or runs over people.

QUALITIES OF EFFECTIVE PASTORAL MINISTERS

The term *pastoral*, as it is used in this book, denotes a minister's ability to relate with people in ways that are personal, caring, and compassionate, and which, in turn, evoke feelings of trust, comfort, and respect from people. Ministers cannot always be pastoral, any more than they can always be competent or effective. Ministers are only human and cannot control all the factors in every situation. However, ministers can work toward becoming more pastoral, competent, and effective in an increasing number of situations with increasingly different kinds of people.

If the minister is psychologically healthy, then he or she is more apt to be pastorally effective. This section will discuss several qualities that effective pastoral ministers seem to share. Each of these qualities is on a continuum; that is, each can be possessed to degrees that are miniscule, moderate, extensive, or not possessed at all.

It is helpful for ministers not only to recognize what these qualities are, but also to understand why they are important and what are the effects when ministers lack these qualities.

A HEALTHY SPIRITUALITY

The first quality that effective pastoral ministers share is a healthy and vibrant spirituality. This means possessing two things: (1) an active prayer life; (2) an assimilated theology.

Effective pastoral ministers have an active prayer life that consists of daily communication with God through talking, meditating, contemplating, and participating in liturgies. Ministers may not substitute good works for prayer any more than a good spouse may substitute hard work for loving communication. If good works remain detached from prayer over a period of time, they can lose their originating purpose, become rote and humanitarian instead of spontaneous and Christian.

The prayer of pastoral ministers cannot simply be a routine performed as part of ministerial self-identity or a duty performed to avoid feeling guilty. Prayer must be engaged in with the same affection, joy, and faithfulness as communication between loving spouses.

Pastoral ministers have a *prayer life*; nonpastoral ministers *say prayers*, and this represents all the difference in the world. Ministers who just "say" prayers separate their prayer from the rest of the day. After their morning prayers, their behavior does not differ from anyone else's, except that they may have a different vocabulary, using words like God, Christ, Church, love, law, and sin. A prayer "life" is much more than saying prayers; it is a theme that permeates daily behaviors in significant, observable ways.

Ministers who have a prayer life are more patient, empathetic, courageous, just, and freeing. They rarely find themselves destructively judging people, because they understand that not everyone has had love and justice in their lives. They seldom lack the courage to stand up to any person or institution which is functioning in ways that are detrimental to others. It is very untypical of them to treat people unjustly, that is, to use them, to be dishonest with them, and to refuse to affirm them when it would be appropriate to do so. They do not capture people with indoctrination, but free them with education. They view Jesus as a good friend whom they want to introduce to their other good friends. They do not fear God, or introduce God to people as one introduces the new foreman on the job.

Effective pastoral ministers also have an assimilated theology (in contrast to having virtually no theology or one that is not assimilated). A minister can be very religious but have no theology that ties together and makes sense out of his or her religious behaviors and teaching. This situation is analogous to a college professor who teaches psychology but has no underlying philosophy that affords direction, substance, and meaning to his individual lectures.

A nonassimilated theology means that a person has studied theology, perhaps has a doctorate in theology, but has not assimilated it into his or her life. Such people are like a person who is a psychologist from nine o'clock to five o'clock but acts quite differently the rest of the time. In other words, their knowledge has not become assimilated into their beings; it has become stuck in their intellects and has not flowed into their hearts and souls. Such ministers may be able to quote Christ, Aquinas, Augustine, Calvin, Francis, Dominic, Luther, Ignatius, and Wesley, but they have not been able to capture the spirit of these figures in their daily behavior.

Ministers wtih an assimilated theology sift it through other, God-given sources of enlightenment, such as psychology, the physical sciences, sociology, anthropology, philosophy, and history. In this way, their theology takes on a depth and an expanse that allows them to grow in all directions—not just vertically— and allows them to have a fuller appreciation of, and empathy toward, the people and the world that God created.

Saying that effective pastoral ministers have an assimilated theology does not mean that they have a private one that has become disconnected from the mainstream of sound theological thought. It simply means that pastoral ministers have a theology that has become *them* and is worn, not like an ill-fitting cloak borrowed from some other person or institution, but like a tailored suit that must be continually altered to fit their ongoing growth.

HELPFUL MOTIVATION

The second quality shared by effective pastoral ministers is that of helpful motivation. Motives flow from needs and move people to act or not to act. Unfortunately, motives are not always conscious. Therefore, people can honestly think, feel, and say that they are acting for one reason when, in fact, they are acting for a very different one. The concurrent problems that this discrepancy causes are more readily observed by others than by the person acting. In reality, however, it is unusual for a motive to be absolutely pure. Most motives are two-dimensional; that is, they flow from both altruistic and self-centered needs. Depending upon a motive's "need" source, this two-dimensionality can be helpful or unhelpful in ministry. Ministerial motives arising out of needs for affection, accomplishment, correctness, and power may serve to demonstrate this dichotomy.

The need to give affection motivates helpful behavior when the affection promotes growth in others and causes joy in oneself. Ministers who share affection in ways that cause people to become more accepting and loving of themselves, more free and courageous, and more accepting and loving of others, are being helpful. The fact that ministers feel good because they are instrumental in this growth is healthy and good.

Problems can occur when ministers give affection as an investment: in order to seduce people into dependent relationships, to convert them to the minister's religious beliefs, to win their affection, or to own and control them. Giving this type of affection is unhelpful and quite possibly damaging.

The need to receive affection is natural and good. Ministers need as much affection (attention, affirmation, intimacy) as anyone else. However, receiving affection as a goal is best left to the minister's personal life; that is, the minister should seek affection from his or her family, friends, and colleagues. When ministers consciously or unconsciously seek to be liked by the people they serve, three problems arise. First, as long as ministers focus on receiving affection, their attention cannot be adequately focused on the people to whom they are supposed to be ministering. Second, when ministers need to be liked more than they need to have integrity, they are vulnerable to the pressures, manipulations, or whims of people, all of which may be inappropriate or damaging. Third, through the process of natural selection, such ministers tend to attract mutually needy people and exclude the psychologically healthy people that every parish so desperately needs.

The need to feel a sense of accomplishment (achievement, success) motivates helpful behavior when it causes a minister to work and relate in ways that cause others to become closer to Jesus, themselves, and one another. If, in the process, ministers feel a personal sense of accomplishment, they should enjoy it and use it to refuel their efforts.

The need to feel a sense of accomplishment can become problematic, however, when it mostly serves the minister's needs for success, praise, and promotion to a more prestigious status. When this is the case, the people become pawns. Sooner or later, they realize the truth of the situation, and become resentful and disinclined to get involved in future Church affairs.

The need to feel special can motivate facilitative behavior when it causes a minister to grow in ways that will increase his or her unique personality, gifts, and values. As the minister grows in this direction, he or she becomes a fuller person and helps others actualize their potential.

The need to be special can create tension, however, when it subtly evolves into a need to feel superior to others; that is, to feel intellectually brighter, morally superior, and spiritually closer to God. This motive will be reflected in the minister's demeanor and will eventually drive people away.

The need to be correct can motivate healthy behavior in ministers when it moves them to become knowledgeable about religion, the Church, and human behavior. The more knowledge they possess, the more effective they can be as religious educators.

The need to be correct can be counterproductive, however, when ministers believe that everything they think is true actually is true, when they cannot tolerate ideas that differ from theirs, and when they cannot admit that they have been in error. When these situations occur, the ministers, as ambassadors of the Church, place it in an incredible light.

Finally, the need to have power can motivate effective behavior in ministers when it causes them to bring about personal, social, and theological change. Positive changes are necessary if the Church and society are to survive and flourish.

The need to be powerful can create difficulties, however, when ministers need to take charge of everything in which they are interested. This motive communicates to people that the minister is the only one who can do things correctly, reduces people to sheep rather than ministers in their own right, and deprives people of considering alternate and, perhaps, more effective ways of accomplishing their goals.

ABSOLUTE HONESTY

The third quality of effective pastoral ministers is absolute honesty. If the Church, through its ministers, is not scrupulously honest, it is no different than any secular institution, except that by pretending to be better (i.e., more honest), it becomes more pernicious than most secular institutions. To possess the quality of honesty, pastoral ministers must conscientiously avoid rationalizations which allow them to ignore, deny, temper, or distort what they know or believe to be true, even when it would be to their temporary advantage to do so.

Honesty means much more than simply not lying to people. It means that pastoral ministers

- tell the whole truth, refusing to hedge in the interests of reducing anxiety in themselves or others;
- disseminate information accurately, without overplaying or underplaying it to make a point or teach a lesson, no matter how "Christian" the point of the lesson;
- tell others of the reasons for asking them to resign, without resorting to lies or half-truths as a way of being "Christian";
- inform the people about financial, political, or ecclesiastical decisions and matters which they have the right to know, without resorting to the well-worn rationalization, "What the people don't know won't hurt them";
- disagree, either publicly or privately, with people who espouse beliefs that run contrary to Christian values, even at the risk of losing respect, support, or friends;

- communicate to authority when they cannot follow a particular teaching or directive, even when it would be more political to be silent;
- choose members for consultative groups (schools or parish boards, boards of directors, etc.) based on the members' competence and not on their willingness to go along with the minister's ideas;
- assign ministers and pastors on the basis of their competence (which includes spirituality) and not simply because it is "their turn," or because there is a slot to fill;
- refuse to teach people that certain acts are inherently sinful when the ministers know full well that an individual's subjective state must be taken into serious consideration when judging the sinfulness of an act;
- refuse to lie or tell half-truths about drugs, sex, or alcohol, even when such dishonesty would motivate people to be more judicious in their behavior;
- refuse to use scriptural passages to buttress their position when exegetes have offered different interpretations that are equally cogent;
- refuse to pretend to know more than they actually do about theology, Scripture, ecclesiology, Church law, psychology, or counseling, even when such pretense would save them embarrassment;
- refuse to tell people that they are better or worse than they are in an effort to be helpful.

All pastoral ministers must be especially cautious with regard to honesty. They must take special care not to slip into a skewed logic that will support dishonesty:

> The Lord is good,
> I am an instrument of the Lord,
> Therefore, everything I do must be good.

Honesty requires strength, courage, humility, and a healthy disregard for advancement and the opinions of others.

Healthy Sensitivity

A fourth quality of effective pastoral ministers is a healthy sensitivity to people and to the nuances of situations. Healthy sensitivity lies at the midpoint between being thin-skinned and thick-skinned.

A thin-skinned minister is easily hurt by the criticisms or oversights of others, and is overburdened by the suffering of others. As a result, these ministers are distracted a good deal of the time by hurt, frustration, resentment, or suffering, which impairs their ability to relate comfortably with others. Moreover, their oversensitivity shows and causes people either to treat them with kid gloves or to stay away from them.

Thick-skinned ministers have a psychological crust to protect themselves from hurt. As a result, they tend to be impervious to the needs and frailties of others and to the emotional climate in social situations. Consequently, they unintentionally hurt people and often behave like a bull in a china shop. Their insensitivity keeps people at a distance and significantly impedes the ministers' ability to be pastorally effective.

Sensitivity is important in ministers because people often communicate their deepest concerns and feelings in veiled forms: an almost imperceptible change in a tone of voice, a flinch in a facial expression, a shift in posture, or a tightening of hands. Most meaningful communication is sensed, not heard. For example, a distraught woman says to a minister, "My son Peter got arrested last night for shoplifting. I just don't know what to do with him. I'm at my wit's end." The less sensitive minister, who may hear what the woman is saying but who fails to sense what she is asking, replies, "Well, let me give you the name of a social service agency where I think you can get some help."

A more sensitive minister, perceiving the woman's feelings of fear, frustration, anger, guilt, confusion, and desperation, says, "You look as though you are filled with all kinds of feelings that would be good for you to get out. I would like it if we could talk for a while, and see if we can't help you feel better so that you can make some clear decisions."

The sensitive minister focuses on the woman who is present, not on her son who is absent. After the woman talks for a while, she may perceive things more clearly and optimistically and may feel that someone genuinely cares about her. It is at this point that the minister can offer her some referral sources.

In the same situation, an overly sensitive minister replies, "Oh, my gosh, that's terrible! How could your son have done such a thing! You poor thing, you must feel terrible! Here, let me drive you home, and we'll talk to him together. Then I'll make an appointment to see him tomorrow. Meanwhile, I'll call a couple of people I know and see if I can get him some professional help. But you need some support, too. Why don't we meet tonight after dinner and see if we can't help you pull yourself together?"

The overly sensitive response creates three problems. First, the minister is nearly as upset as the woman, so the blind is leading the blind. Secondly, the minister's anxiety causes the woman to become more anxious. Instead of thinking how best to solve her problem, she is wondering how to extricate herself from the minister. Thirdly, by the time the minister is finished dealing with the woman, the minister will be exhausted and virtually useless for the rest of the day.

Ministers must be cautious with regard to the quality of their sensitivity. Many begin their ministry as very sensitive people, but as they experience daily suffering, criticism, and apathy, they laminate their hearts so that they do not feel as much. They become more businesslike and less empathetic. They say all the right words but lack all the right feelings that are supposed to go with the words. Although the lamination around their hearts protects them from pain, it also protects them from experiencing warmth, love, joy, and beauty, the very experiences that would help them also experience pain without becoming injured.

GENTLE STRENGTH

Gentle strength is the fifth quality possessed by effective pastoral ministers. Ministers can be both gentle and strong at the same time. The quality of gentle strength is necessary for effective pastoral ministry for several reasons.

It is important because ministers must stand up for true Christian values in a world, and sometimes (paradoxically) in a Church, that would find other values more diplomatic or expedient. In holding forth these values, ministers risk being scorned and rejected. To decline to proclaim values such as love, justice, freedom, and honesty is weak and nonministerial. At the same time, to proclaim these values in a harsh, intimidating manner is unchristian. Representing Christian values publicly must be done with a gentleness that flows from genuine concern rather than from fear or anger, and with a strength that denotes commitment and conviction.

Gentle strength is important because it is the basis of assertiveness. Gentle strength lies at the midpoint between being unassertive and aggressive. Ministers must be able to present their ideas, feelings, beliefs, and values in straightforward, clear ways; and they must be able to remain steadfast in the face of manipulation, unrealistic expectations, or impossible requests.

Gentle strength is also the basis for resistance to stress. Effective ministers are involved in many areas of responsibility, and this involvement can cause stress, sometimes great stress. Ministers who are gentle but not sufficiently strong may become worn down or bowled over by stress. Ministers who are strong but lack gentleness may be ungentle with themselves, failing to protect themselves from stress, and unable to perceive the internal clues of pending physical or psychological problems.

Gentle strength denotes an ability to be flexible when situations merit it. Unmitigated and unswerving strength is not always a virtue and, in fact, can be a liability in a minister. For example, there are times when moral judgments must take a backseat to gentleness, compassion, and understanding; and there are times when it is appropriate for ministers to accede to the beliefs, the wishes, and the values of others.

Sometimes ministers must make difficult decisions that cause anxiety or unhappiness in some people. Because effective ministers are strong, they do not shirk making these decisions. On the other hand, because effective ministers are gentle, they are careful to make decisions which reflect sensitivity to the people and the issues involved.

Gentle strength is also necessary for perseverance, a quality that is often called upon in ministry. Because of human nature, ministers are often faced with people and projects that cause them to feel frustrated and, at times, discouraged. However, a gentle strength allows ministers to keep trying to minister in ways that are unabrasive and increasingly fruitful.

Finally, a gentle strength allows ministers to extricate themselves from damaging relationships and unworkable situations. Their strength allows ministers to retreat, even though it will upset others; their gentleness allows them to withdraw in the most painless ways possible.

Ministers who are too gentle may be that way because of their personalities, because they do not want to cause anxiety in themselves or others, or because they view gentleness as a Christian virtue and strength (assertiveness, confrontation) as unchristian, even though there is ample evidence of Christ's being equally gentle and strong.

Ministers who are too strong may be that way because of their personalities, because gentleness is viewed as weakness and thus creates anxiety within them, or because they have overidentified with the strength of Christ and underidentified with his gentleness.

Ministers who are too gentle are inclined to be manipulated, nonconfrontive of people and situations that should be confronted, and nonassertive. Ministers who are too strong think they can muscle people into Christian behavior with intellectual assaults, emotional tirades, and theological threats. In addition, they are insensitive to people's frailties and to the nuances of delicate situations. This causes others to view such ministers as threats or as objects of derision.

II. GENUINELY FREEING

Being a person who is genuinely freeing is the sixth quality of effective pastoral ministers. Ministers who are genuinely freeing allow others to exercise freedom of will and freedom of choice. Freedom is a basic Christian value. A good deal of Christ's message deals with freeing people from the inappropriate and unhealthy restraints of the law, politics, religious myths, families, social mores, and worship.

In a Christian context, freedom does not mean unbridled freedom; it does not mean that people are free to behave in ways that are destructive; it does not imply that all restraints are inappropriate or unhealthy. Rather, freedom means that people are free to make their choices and decisions within the broader boundaries of justice and love. Effective ministers realize that often there is not just one path to justice and love, and that the path a particular person takes may not be the one the minister would choose. However, when such a situation occurs—and it may occur with some frequency—effective ministers stand by the person and assist him or her in any ways in which the ministers feel comfortable; and that assistance does not necessarily imply that the ministers would have taken the same path. Perhaps one of the acid tests of truly pastoral ministers is that they stand by and help a person even when they may not agree with the person's decision.

Pastoral ministers *invite* people to follow them toward Jesus. It is not a casual invitation ("I don't really care if you follow me or not"); but neither is it a direct order ("Follow me to Christ or else you will be doomed"). Ministers understand that many paths lead to the Kingdom and that they represent but one of those paths. In addition to the theological reasons for inviting people to follow Christ, there are equally sound psychological ones. A kind yet concerned invitation is far more likely to attract people than is a command performance. Ministers who abide by a "take it or else" approach are likely to repulse people who, in a modern democratic society, generally bolt at being told that they *must* do something, or they will attract a frightened, resentful following, which is not what Christ had in mind.

It seems that ministers who exert their wills on the people rather than allow people to use their own wills are not working as much in the service of Jesus as in the service of themselves.

They have overidentified with their message, and they feel that to reject it is to reject them. Their attempts to convert people to the Word are veiled attempts to convert people to themselves, much as possessive parents are less concerned about their children's welfare than they are concerned about keeping their children dependent upon them.

Pastoral ministers do not use freedom as a manipulative ploy to draw people to them. This very subtle, sometimes unconscious, dynamic happens even when a concerned, loving person uses the offer of freedom to trap people. This dynamic is based on the message, "I'll prove to you how really good and loving I am by giving you complete freedom to leave me in order to follow someone else or to follow your own lights." The hope is that the person will realize how absolutely good, loving, and unselfish the minister is, and will feel even more attracted and indebted to him or her.

True pastoral ministers free people to be absolutely honest with them. People know that they can disagree with their minister and that they can decline an invitation to work or relate socially with him or her without damaging the relationship. Unfreeing ministers send the message, "I will be hurt or angry if you don't agree with everything I say or do, or if you say no to me." People who received this message either cater to the minister—even when it may not be in their best interests, and even when it breeds resentment—or they stay away from the minister because they do not want to get trapped.

If ministers feel compelled to bring people to Jesus because they feel they have been mandated by God to do so or because bringing people to Jesus is an integral part of their personal sense of self-worth, they will feel the same intense pressure as does a salesman who must meet quotas and deadlines, and the effect on them is the same. Ministers will become high-pressure salespeople for Christ, treating people like potential customers who must be manipulated, seduced, loved, and threatened into buying the product. If the person refuses to "buy," the minister feels like a failure and makes the person feel foolish or doomed.

Acting this way is both unchristian and ineffective. A more valid, less pressurized attitude would be to view oneself as a tour guide who can lead people to some beautiful places. If people would prefer to launch out on their own, they are freely allowed that option and are always welcome to return to the tour if they choose. In addition, the tour guide (minister) does not define his or her worth by *how many* people he or she gets to sign up for the tour, but by how he or she treats people, whether or not they choose to follow him or her.

VII. UNCONDITIONALLY PRESENT

The quality of being unconditionally present to people means that whatever decisions people make and however far from the Kingdom their paths wander, the effective pastoral minister will always be at their side, attempting to shed light and bring assistance.

It does not mean that ministers must unconditionally love all people, because this seems to be terribly unrealistic, at least by my definition of love. But ministers can be always present, ready to help people in all ways but those that would cause people to stray from goodness.

Ministers shed the light of faith, and when people get lost despite the light, ministers go out and look for them. Ministers also realize that there are many paths that lead to the Kingdom, and the fact that a person chooses an unpopular one does not necessarily mean that he or she is less of a Christian.

Ministers are in a particularly good position to be unconditionally present to people becuase it is often very difficult for loved ones to do so with a child, a spouse, a parent, or a close friend who makes choices or behaves in ways that are perceived as wrong, destructive, selfish, or sinful. Loved ones are often so hurt, threatened, confused, or guilty about the person's behavior that they must disassociate themselves from the person to avoid being overcome by anguish. A minister, who is typiclly less emotionally involved in the situation, is freer to stand by the person, just as the physician is better able to treat a child than is the child's parent.

To be able to be present unconditionally, ministers must separate themselves from the "rock throwers," that is, from those Christians who, because of their own unresolved conflicts, throw rocks at sinners or at people whom they perceive to be sinners. Ministers cannot be in a position of throwing rocks and then rushing to stem the bleeding caused by the very rocks that they and their fellow Christians have thrown. By the same token, ministers must be willing to get hit by some rocks as they minister to the victims of the rock throwers.

This is not easy—to be stoned for no other reason than that one is helping a fallen Christian who cannot get up because other Christians are pelting him or her with rocks. Being a rock thrower is easy. It is easy to denounce abortion. It is much more difficult to help a woman who has decided to have an abortion through the abortion and to help her live the rest of her life as fully as she can.

It is easy to denounce premarital sex. It is much more challenging to help a young woman who is pregnant outside of marriage and the boy who has fathered the child live through and after this difficult peiod in the most effective, helpful, and Christian way.

It is easy to denounce divorce. It is much more arduous to help people live and perhaps even grow through a divorce so that they can become fuller people and more committed Christians.

It is easy to denounce homosexuals. It is much more difficult to help a homosexual to strive to become a better Christian, despite obstacles that fellow Christians place before him or her.

It is easy to denounce people who have left the more established kinds of ministry. It is harder to remain with them, offering the support they sometimes need to pave a different path toward the Kingdom.

Toward sinners and people they perceive to be sinners, rock throwers harbor attitudes such as "They should be left to stew in their own juices," or "They made their bed, now let them lie in it," or "They deserve to get their comeuppance." Pastoral ministers do not subscribe to these attitudes.

Ministers have all they can do to be helpful to, and compassionate with, people who are suffering, just as ambulance attendants at an accident have all they can do to treat the victims. And, just as ambulance attendants leave it to the courts to judge who caused the accident, ministers do the psychological and spiritual resuscitation and leave the judging to God.

When the rock throwers return home to the warmth and comfort of their righteousness, the minister remains behind to begin the arduous, unpopular, and sometimes thankless task of being unconditionally present.

INTELLECTUALLY COMPETENT

Whatever facet of ministry a person is involved in, he or she needs to be competent to carry out its responsibilities. This does not necessarily mean that ministers must be highly educated or possess academic degrees. Some very competent ministers do not possess a good deal of formal education, while some less than competent ministers have the highest academic degrees attainable. Whatever their formal education, competent ministers seem to possess the following qualities.

They possess a breadth of knowledge that covers the area in which they teach. Their knowledge is not inordinately limited by their intelligence, personal biases, aversion to study, insecurity, overconfidence, or laziness.

They do not learn their Christianity by rote and pass it along to others in a parrotlike fashion. They sift the information through a process of critical thinking, discussion, argumentation, and meditation, allowing it to seep from their intellects into their psyches and souls so that it becomes an integral part of them. This process constitutes the critical difference between having knowledge and being knowledgeable.

Competent ministers are intellectually growing. This means that effective ministers continually study and learn. They keep up with the religious literature as conscientiously as physicians, attorneys, and psychologists keep current with the literature in their fields. Ministers are never too experienced, busy, tired, contented, or old to learn a good deal more than they know. They realize that the more they know and understand, the more they can grow and help others grow.

Ministers are intellectually flexible and are willing to try new methodologies in order to increase their effectiveness. They are not anchored to one theory, philosophy, or technique by which they live or die. They recognize that what works with one person or group may be a disaster with another.

Thus, competent ministers are willing to listen to the people's needs and suggestions and to modify their teaching accordingly, rather than having a plan that they foist on people, regardless of whether or not it is suitable for them.

Ministers are intellectually democratic and search everywhere for truth. They read the works and attend the workshops of other denominations. They study other fields, such as psychology, sociology, philosophy, anthropology, and biology, in an attempt to augment and strengthen their understanding of themselves, others, life, and God. They are open to any ideas that are helpful, whether they come from liberals, moderates, or conservatives, from women or men, or from ordained or nonordained people. They do not possess a "private club" mentality, which holds that anyone or anything outside of their group could have nothing worthwhile to offer.

Competent ministers are intellectually creative. Their idea of ministry is to stimulate themselves and others to think for themselves. They do not simply record what they read and hear, then play back the tape for their audiences, who, in turn, replay it for family and friends. Intellectually competent ministers digest what they read and hear, and they modify it with their own ideas, perceptions, and experiences. In one situation, the modification may be to taper what they read and hear, and in another situation, it may be to add to it. In other words, such ministers do not discount the fact that they themselves can be a source of knowledge, and they do not rely solely on others for enlightenment. By the same principle, they stimulate others to think for themselves by questioning, challenging, and encouraging others to add their own wisdom, creating a second force.

Competent ministers are intellectually discerning. They carefully evaluate what they read and hear, and measure it against logic, common sense, objectivity, what others say, and their own experiences. They do not believe something simply because someone in authority proclaimed it, or someone they admire believes it, or someone holy said it. On the other hand, they do not automatically discount something because someone in authority proclaimed it, or someone they don't like believes it, or someone unholy said it. Thus, by the same principle, such ministers are discerning in what they teach and preach, being prudent and careful not to say things that could be easily misconstrued by their audiences. For example, what a minister says to a group of middle-aged adults may be imprudent to say to a group of teenagers, and vice versa.

Competent ministers are intellectually honest. This means that pastoral ministers appreciate the limitations inherent in knowing God. Therefore, they do not pretend to have knowledge about the nature and workings of God that, in reality, no human being possesses or will ever possess. Ministers may possess great faith and hope in God, but they do not confuse this with great knowledge. In their teaching and preaching, they are careful to indicate clearly the differences between theological facts, theories, hypotheses, interpretations, educated guesses, myths, uncertainties, legitimate hopes, and wishful thinking.

Because they recognize the great abyss between the enormity of God and their own severely limited human intellect, ministers feel completely comfortable admitting theological ignorance, confusion, and doubt. They place their integrity above all else and do not teach and preach precepts or directives with which, in good conscience, they disagree.

APPROACHABILITY

The ninth, and final, quality of effective pastoral ministers is approachability. It is important that people feel comfortable with, and free to approach, a minister. A minister's effectiveness is in direct proportion to his or her proximity to the people. Ministers can communicate one of the three following messages relevant to approachability: (1) "I am someone with whom you can share your being"; (2) "I am someone you'd want to officiate at your wedding or invite to supper, but not someone with whom you could share your innermost self"; or (3) "I am someone you would prefer to avoid, except when transacting necessary business." The approachable minister must develop qualities that allow him or her to speak only the first message.

Approachable ministers seem to share the following qualities. First of all, they are not afraid to let people come close to them. And when they allow that closeness, they are not afraid that they will become attached to, exploited, trapped, or found wanting by the other person. They have sufficient love in their lives and enough self-control that they will not become attached. They have sufficient strength and assertiveness that they would not allow themselves to be misused. And they have sufficient self-confidence and self-worth that, whether or not they are found wanting, they can handle it with equanimity.

Secondly, approachable ministers are perceived as warm, understanding, and accepting. Warm means gentle and affectionate, in contrast to rigid and distant. Understanding means that the ministers are able to empathize with people, in contrast to perceiving them as silly, stupid, or weak. Accepting means that ministers invite the other into their lives as he or she is, in contrast to denying entrance until the person meets certain criteria.

Thirdly, approachable ministers speak with people; they do not preach at them. They are not programmed by theological tapes, but are real, unique, spontaneous people who defy stereotyping. Thus, they do not have pat answers—many times they have no answers—just an informed willingness to help. They do have a sense of humor and humility that helps them keep both themselves and their work in a healthy perspective, which precludes them taking themselves too seriously.

Fourth, approachable ministers recognize the difference between what is real and what is ideal, and they do not act as if the two were synonymous or even very close. Thus, they know the

difference between heaven and earth and do not expect mere
mortals to think and behave like angels. They are close to God
but down-to-earth, so that anyone can understand, challenge,
and feel comfortable with them.

Fifth, approachable ministers are well aware of their humanity—of their frailties, weaknesses, and failures. This exquisite
awareness of their dark side precludes even the slightest inclina-
tion toward pretension, arrogance, or superciliousness, all of
which are unbecoming in any person with insight and much less
so in a minister. Because they are aware of their humanity, ministers can deal comfortably with the humanity of others without
being shocked or repulsed by it. Since these ministers allow their
humanity to show, they do not project an idealized image that
scares off others.

Finally, approachable ministers balance their intellect and
emotions. That is, they do not operate mostly on the basis of
thoughts, principles, laws, syllogisms, and deductive or inductive
reasoning. Rather, they realize that there is much more to life
than law and logic and that few people have been drawn closer
to God by an idea, no matter how noble or correct. On the other
hand, ministers do not overwork their emotions. They do not allow feelings of love, hope, happiness, or fervor to override the
unpleasant aspects of reality in themselves and others. Nor do
they allow feelings of sadness, anger, frustration, or discouragement to override the positive aspects of reality in themselves and
others.

Unfortunately, ministers' religious training can sometimes be
so concerned with dogma, law, logic, absolutes, moral judgments, and perfection that ministers may evolve from it acting
like religious robots. They do all the right things in the wrong
ways: they talk to people without communicating with them;
they counsel people without helping them; they teach people
without educating them; they rub against people without touching them; they love people without liking them; they lead prayers without praying; and they live without life.

Approachable ministers recognize that they are human beings

with both intellect and emotions. That combination, though not always synchronized, constitutes a powerful instrument of psychological and spiritual growth for the ministers themselves and for others as well.

Ministers who lack the above pastoral qualities are not good for the soul. Either they are not invited into the souls of people, or if they are, they do damage that could have eternal ramifications. No minister is perfectly pastoral, but it is important for every minister to work continuously toward that goal.

Effective pastoral ministers are good for the soul. They are invited into people's souls and have a strengthening, freeing, and peaceful effect as they work within the depths of the person. Although not everyone needs a physician or a psychologist, everyone needs a *pastoral* minister, whether or not he or she recognizes it.

2. Ministers as Facilitators of Growth

A necessary part of being an effective and pastoral minister is to have at least a working knowledge of human behavior and pastoral counseling. Most ministers today realize that the psyches and the souls of people are so intertwined that each must be addressed.

Therefore, in order to avoid "the blind leading the blind" syndrome, it is important for ministers to have an informed view of personality dynamics and pastoral counseling so that they will be more of a help than a hindrance to people. Ministers who rely mostly on armchair psychology are apt to create more problems than they solve, regardless of the soundness of their theology. Ministers need not be professional psychologists or counselors in order to be helpful, but they should know enough about human behavior to be reasonably helpful to the people who come to them, even if it means knowing when to make a professional referral.

It is in this spirit that this chapter deals with the goals of helping people, the typical problems people bring to ministers, some destructive myths regarding helping people, some pitfalls ministers can encounter, and some cautions with respect to pastoral counseling.

THE GOALS OF HELPING

Since the vast majority of counseling situations ministers encounter last between one and ten visits, the theme of this chapter will deal with short-term counseling. The goals of short-term counseling are fivefold.

5 goals

First, short-term counseling tries to help people view themselves, their concern(s), and others more realistically so that they are in a better position to deal with or change the situation which has caused them to seek counseling. People often overestimate or underestimate the seriousness of their concerns; hence it is the minister's role to help the person objectify the situation. People also often idealize or inappropriately devalue the significant others in their lives, creating unnecessary problems for themselves.

Second, short-term counseling seeks to help people get in touch with their emotions, understand them, ventilate them, and use them to begin new behaviors and discontinue old, less adaptive behaviors. Typical emotions that people bring to ministers are hurt, fear, anger, guilt, sadness, loneliness, and confusion. People also bring emotions of hope, or they would not bother to seek help.

The third goal of short-term counseling is to help people relate socially with others in ways that increase their need fulfillment, that is, in ways that allow people to feel more secure, loved, and esteemed. People who seek a minister's help are often experiencing a problematic, nonfulfilling relationship with a significant other (e.g., a parent, a spouse, a close friend).

Fourth, short-term counseling endeavors to help people develop a sound and healthy moral value system and to help them use it in ways that promote moral and religious, as well as overall, growth. People often get themselves into trouble by losing sight of their moral and religious values. They may have slipped in the areas of honesty, charity, self-transcendence, humility, spiritual purpose-in-life, prayer, etc.

The fifth goal of short-term counseling is to help people gain the courage needed to make the decisions necessary for growth, even when those decisions may temporarily increase anxiety. Many people who seek help want other people or situations to change so that they will feel happy. Those people need to realize that their ultimate happiness is contingent on the decisions that only they themselves can make. As long as they are unwilling to take new steps, they cannot realistically expect to feel better.

It is important for ministers to understand the goals of helping so that they will have a general plan of action when people seek their help. It is likely that the problem brought by an individual to a minister will fit into, and can be solved by simply applying, one or more of the above five counseling goals. The more ministers understand the goals of short-term counseling, the less they will need to ask themselves, "What in the world am I supposed to do with this person?"

PROBLEMS PEOPLE BRING TO MINISTERS

Basically there are two kinds of problems that people bring to ministers: (1) immediate, disconnected problems; (2) immediate, connected problems. An immediate, disconnected problem is one which has *recently come into existence and is disconnected from any ongoing, basic problem(s)*. An immediate, connected problem is one that has *recently been precipitated but is connected to a basic, ongoing problem(s)*. It is sometimes difficult to tell which type of problem a person has without knowing something about the person. For example, a woman comes to a minister and states that her problem is that her husband is drinking too much. If her husband is actually drinking too much, that is, if his drinking is significantly interfering with his work or his home life, and if the woman is not subconsciously instigating his drinking for her own purposes, then the woman's problem is immediate. It significantly distresses her at present, and is disconnected from any basic, ongoing problem that is a part of her behavior.

A second woman may approach a minister with the same complaint. However, this woman has a basic, ongoing problem—a strong need to control the behavior of the people whom she most loves (husband, children, parents, closest friend). She has preconceived ideas as to how people should behave and what will make them happy. She prescribes these behaviors in subtle or obvious ways for the people about whom she cares the most. When these people behave contrary to her prescriptions, she becomes anxious and angry and struggles to regain control of their behavior.

The woman seeks the support of a minister because the more she tries to control her husband's drinking (which, in fact, is not excessive but which she detests), the more he drinks. She finally becomes so frustrated and feels so helpless that she enlists the aid of a minister to help her gain control of her husband's behavior. She tells the minister that her husband's drinking is causing her and the children to lose respect for him. In fact, she loses respect for her husband whenever he behaves in any ways that are normal and natural for him but contrary to her prescription. The children are upset only because she is upset and is magnifying her husband's drinking into a family stress.

In the first situation, the focus of helping is on an attempt to get the husband involved with his wife in a program to increase and support whatever motivation he has to admit to and work on his drinking problem. If the husband has no such motivation, then the focus would be to help the wife and children deal with the situation in the most appropriate and constructive way. The focus in the second situation is on an attempt to help the wife recognize that her current distress is only a manifestation of a deeper, ongoing problem which creates unnecessary anguish for her and the people she most loves. If she can be helped to get in touch with this dynamic and understand its negative consequences, she is in a position to work on changing it.

It is critically important for ministers to make a distinction between the two types of problems and not to confuse one with the other. If a minister assumes that all problems are immediate and disconnected, he or she will be of no help to people whose problems are actually immediate and connected. If a minister assumes that all problems are immediate and connected, then he or she will be of no help, and, in fact, may be a source of agitation to people whose problems are immediate and disconnected.

Because it seems that the majority of problems people bring to ministers are immediate and connected, the following discussion will deal with basic, ongoing (connected) problems that commonly underlie the immediate problems that ministers encounter.

FEAR OF INTIMACY

Many people are fearful of psychological intimacy, that is, of relating in ways that are profoundly warm, open, trusting, and vulnerable. People who have been hurt or have witnessed others being hurt as a result of intimacy often perceive intimacy as both attractive and threatening at the same time. These individuals avoid intimacy by unconsciously constructing barriers in a relationship. Then they lament their loneliness and blame others for being overbearing, insensitive, too passive, or disinterested. However, the negative behavior of others is actually the effect and not the cause of the person's problem.

People who are afraid of intimacy approach the minister with the question "How can I get people to be more intimate with me?" The real question is, "How can I recognize my fear of intimacy and work to diminish it?"

SUPPRESSED FEELINGS

Some people suppress their feelings for the sake of peace. They rationalize their suppression by assuring themselves that the issues that aroused their feelings are minor and that the tension that would be caused by communicating their concerns would not be worth it. These people assure themselves that things will get better, which precludes any action on their part.

However, the suppressed feelings of hurt, anger, frustration, and confusion fester and gradually cause a state of psychological toxicity. Usually, the increasing symptoms of toxicity (depression, anxiety, insomnia), or "the last straw," fall on the person's already overburdened back, and bring the person to the minister.

The questions these people bring to ministers are, "Why am I so depressed lately?" or "How do I call back all those terrible things I said when I exploded?" The real question is, "Why am I so reluctant to share each significant feeling as I experience it, so that psychological straws weaken me to the point of depression or explosion?"

THE "GOT TO HAVE IT OR I'LL DIE" SYNDROME

This syndrome is exemplified by people who target other people or situations as keys to their survival and happiness. These people feel that they *must have a* particular person as a friend, a fiance, or a spouse; that they *must get* a particular job, promotion, award, or into a particular school. They are often unwilling to compromise and tend to put all their hopes on one person or situation. Because these people often manage to get what they want, they are happy most of the time. But when something they want and think they need for survival and happiness eludes their grasp, they experience a combination of desolation, outrage, and panic.

These people approach a minister with the questions, "How am I going to get what I want, even though I've been told I can't have it?" or "How am I going to live without him/her/it?" The real question, however, is, "How can I both recognize that there is no one person or thing upon which my survival and happiness rests, and also learn to live peacefully with the fact that I'm not going to get something simply because I deeply want it?"

THE NEED TO CHANGE PEOPLE

Some people see a beautiful but imperfect house and buy it with the idea of remodeling it. Some people see a beautiful but imperfect person, such as a friend, a spouse, a child, or a business partner, and "buy" the person with the idea of remodeling him or her. When a person acts in this way, he or she is faced with two immediate problems. First, people are not houses. People will not allow themselves to be remodeled unless they see the good in remodeling and volitionally agree to strive toward that good. Secondly, the desired person's "imperfections" may exist more in the eyes of the beholder than in reality; hence there is no need for remodeling.

Stress arises when the remodeler gradually discovers that the person he or she "bought" is not going to change, even though a lot has been invested in the idea that the person would change.

When this realization finally becomes clear, the distressed remodeler comes to a minister asking, "How can I get him (her) to
change so that we'll be happy?" The question that should be
asked is, "How and when will I learn that I can't change people,

and what is this fact going to do to my current relationship with
the person whom I wanted to change?"

THE INABILITY OR UNWILLINGNESS TO DIRECT ONE'S LIFE

A person lacking the ability or will to direct his or her own life is
like a rudderless ship that either drifts with the current or gets
blown off course by prevailing winds (viz., the needs and values
of significant others). A rudderless psyche may be the result of
one (or more) of three causes: no clear sense of direction; insuffi-
cient psychological strength to follow through on one's sense of
direction; or an unwillingness to assume responsibility for one's
decisions. People lacking direction are unable to declare: "This is
what I want, need, and value. What I want, need, and value is
appropriate, good, and just. If I can get what I want, need, and
value, I will remain in this relationship or situation, and if I can't,
I will have to go elsewhere for it." Instead, the person with the
rudderless psyche states: "I'll be whoever you want me to be and
go wherever you want me to go. If it works out to my advantage,
that will be fine. If I arrive at a bad place, I will be depressed, be
angry, and blame you."

It is only when these people arrive at a bad place that they are
likely to approach a minister with the question, "How do I get
out of this mess?" The question they need to ask, however, is,
"How did I get myself into this mess, and how will I see to it that
I take charge of my life in the future?"

THE "I CAN GET AWAY WITH IT" SYNDROME

People suffering from this syndrome gamble but do not expect to
lose. There is a slogan among criminals: "Don't commit the crime
if you can't do the time." The idea behind the slogan is that one
must be prepared to take the consequences when gambling with
life. People gamble in many ways: by cheating (on exams, in-

come tax, etc.); by having extramarital affairs; by assuming that the people they treat poorly will never be in a position to retaliate; by risking financial investments; by driving too fast or while under the influence of alcohol or drugs; by working too hard; by eating too much and exercising too little; by letting psychological stresses accumulate without dealing with them; by being dishonest with people; by putting all their eggs in one basket; by having premarital sex without using birth control; by ignoring loved ones; by waiting until the last minute to prepare for exams or projects; by committing themselves to people or projects without proper consideration; by making large purchases (houses, cars) that they hope to be able to pay for at a later date; etc.

There are many colloquialisms that describe these behaviors: "Having one's cake and eating it too"; "Burning the candle at both ends"; "Stealing from Peter to pay Paul"; "Playing both ends against the middle."

People involved in this syndrome love to gamble, but they cannot tolerate losing. It is only when they lose that they seek the help of a minister, asking the question, "How am I going to cut my losses?" The question they need to ask is, "How and when will I learn to stop gambling with life and make only investments that are more likely to pay psychologically and spiritually healthy dividends?"

THE TENDENCY TO IGNORE UNPLEASANT REALITY

People who ignore unpleasant reality have conveniently located blind spots, so that they do not see things that would—and should—create anxiety within them. They work on the principle that if one does not see something, it does not exist, and if it does not exist, it does not have to be faced and dealt with. Their family and friends often see the reality that these individuals refuse to see. However, these significant others often may not point out this reality because they fear the reaction it might elicit, or if and when they do point out the reality, it is denied by the person who does not want to see it.

The blind spot of persons who tend to ignore reality may be in relation to themselves (their abrasiveness or destructive behavior), in relation to their spouse (drinking, unfaithfulness), in relation to their children (lying, poor achievement), or in relation to their work (declining business, personnel problems). Unfortunately, when these problems do exist, they cannot be wished out of existence. They incubate and grow until they can no longer be denied. It is at this point that the person contacts a minister and asks, "What do I do now?" A better question would be, "Why didn't I see this happening a year or two ago?"

Of course, ministers cannot ignore the questions that flow from the immediate problem or crisis. But if the person is going to receive any lasting help—in contrast to temporary support—the minister must introduce him or her to the basic, ongoing problem.

In summary, it is helpful for ministers to be aware, first of all, that they should place their ability to be helpful in a realistic perspective; that is, they should neither underestimate nor overestimate their helping abilities. Of course, it is possible for a minister to help people in a significant (which does not mean miraculous) way in only one visit. Many people can look back on their lives and see instances in which they met or heard someone only once, and whatever the person conveyed, either verbally or attitudinally, left a lasting, helpful impression.

However, other people, either because of deep problems or weak motivation to change, will not seem to benefit even from several visits with a minister. A helpful analogy for ministers to keep in mind when dealing with such cases is that of a farmer faced with barren ground. For plants to grow in barren ground entails a five-step process: tilling the ground, adding nutrients, planting seeds, watering, and providing a nurturing environment. Working through these five steps is not always very gratifying for the farmer, but he or she knows that lacking any one of the steps, growth will never occur. In like manner, ministers are often asked to do only some tilling, or to spread some nutrients, or to plant some seeds, or to do some irrigation. They often never see the end result of their labor, which may not occur until years later. But ministers should realize that if they do not do their part in the process, growth may never occur.

This kind of "piecework" often is not very gratifying and sometimes appears to be a waste of time, especially when counselees convey to the minister that they have wasted their time by consulting him or her. Therefore, it is necessary for ministers to transcend the need for immediate results and gratification and to realize the important part they play in the overall picture of psychological and spiritual growth.

It is also important for ministers not to overestimate their ability or to exceed their competence in attempting to help people. Just as there is a great difference between the competencies needed to treat a scraped knee, to do cardiopulmonary resuscitation, or to perform major surgery, so, too, there are concomitant levels of competency needed to help people with problems that vary in severity.

Some people harbor a dangerous myth that in trying to help someone they may not do any good, but they cannot do any harm. While these people would never attempt to perform a heart bypass operation, they fearlessly attempt to perform a comparable operation on a person's psyche. An important principle for ministers to keep in mind is that to the degree that good can be done, harm can be done. This is true in any field, including the area of attempting to help people who have psychological and spiritual problems. Professional counselors and psychotherapists spend between four and eight years on postgraduate study and getting practical experience learning to help people. What they spend years studying and practicing cannot be learned naturally; nor can good intentions and common sense be substituted for it. Therefore, it is important for ministers to recognize their levels of competence and be willing to refer people who need more help than the minister can offer to more competent and experienced professionals.

DESTRUCTIVE MYTHS ABOUT HELPING OTHERS

As is true with many human endeavors, there are several destructive myths with regard to helping people. When ministers believe these myths to be true, their attempts to help people will be superficial, at best, and damaging, at worst. For this reason, it is important to demythologize some commonly held beliefs about helping people, so that ministers can be truly helpful and avoid wasting people's time or damaging them. This section will discuss seven myths which can interfere with effective ministry.

Myth I: Love, Good Intentions, and Common Sense Are All You Need

Love, as the term is used in this myth, means demonstrating care, warmth, affirmation, and support. There is a time for this kind of love, but there is also a time for a different kind of love, one that is demonstrated in confronting, challenging, and setting limits. Both affirming and challenging love are necessary to help people grow.

Good intentions, like affirming love, are necessary to help people, but they are only a beginning. Added to good intentions must be the personal qualities, academic knowledge, and professional skills necessary to help people grow psychologically and spiritually. Good intentions alone in a minister are no more helpful than, and are as potentially damaging as, good intentions in a teacher or a surgeon.

Common sense is also a good place to start, but a poor place to finish. Many things that common sense has held to be true about behavior have proven to be untrue. Moreover, common sense is not always common. For example, a minister's common sense tells her or him that a woman should leave her husband who beats her. However, what is common sense to the minister makes absolutely no sense to the woman, her husband, or their five children. Therefore, it will take far more than the minister's common sense to help this family.

Myth II: People Define Their Problems Accurately

Some people define their problems accurately, but many do not. People can be quite intelligent in many areas of their lives but lack the psychological insight necessary to view the cause and the nature of their problems accurately.

People often misidentify their problems in the following ways. First, they confuse their symptoms with their problems. They define their problem as depression, anxiety, loneliness, or confusion, when these behaviors are often but the side effects of deeper issues. For example, depression could be caused by an unexpressed seething resentment toward one or more significant others which is repressed or which the person is afraid to communicate. General anxiety (tension, insomnia, inability to concentrate) may stem from fears or guilts of which the person is unaware or is only partially aware. Loneliness may be self-induced, caused by a negative self-concept or latent resentment toward people. Confusion may be self-perpetuated in order to help the person avoid facing unpleasant reality squarely. It is important, therefore, that ministers help people differentiate between the smoke and the fire so that they can receive the maximum amount of insight and help.

Secondly, people often define their problems as being caused by someone else. Husbands would be happy if it were not for their wives; employees would be happy if it were not for their bosses; and teenagers would be happy if it were not for their parents. People often fail to recognize how they themselves are a part, and sometimes a large part, of the problem. Until they do so, there can be no solution.

Thirdly, people often define their problems as being caused by situations. They blame their race, sex, religion, age, marital status, job, genes, socioeconomic level, and the past for their current problems. While each of these factors may, in some instances, contribute to a person's stress, they rarely, if ever, are the sufficient cause of personal problems.

To be a sufficient cause, everyone who experiences the situation that the troubled person is experiencing would necessarily have to develop a similar personal problem. Ministers need to be aware that although people cannot always choose their environments or situations, they are always free to choose how they perceive them, how they will react to them, and whether to remain in the situations or to leave them.

MYTH III: MOST PEOPLE JUST NEED ADVICE AND ENCOURAGEMENT

Some people just need some advice and a little encouragement, but most people need much more than this. By the time a person approaches a minister for help, he or she often has heard more advice and received more encouragement than the minister could offer in ten visits. The high school boy knows that he should try harder in school; the high school girl knows that she should stop using drugs; the unemployed man knows that he should be looking for jobs instead of watching television all day. For a minister to tell these people what they already know and to encourage them to change their behavior would be abrasively redundant.

These people need to understand what hurts, fears, angers, guilts, or loneliness cause them to behave in destructive ways, and they need to trust someone in order to talk about and objectify these feelings. These people need to diminish the strength of these hurtful feelings by understanding them and placing them in a realistic perspective. They then need to replace them with more positive feelings, such as self-esteem, trust in others, and hope.

In the absence of this process, simple advice and encouragement can be as dangerous as advising a nonswimmer to jump into a pool. The pool may be only four feet deep to the person giving the advice and encouragement, but it seems twenty feet deep to the person who is not yet ready to try this new behavior.

MYTH IV: YOU SHOULD ENCOURAGE PEOPLE TO VENTILATE THEIR FEELINGS

Sometimes it is helpful to encourage people to ventilate their feelings, but at other times it is not helpful. Emotional ventilation can be helpful when people have bottled-up, intense feelings and need to feel, clarify, and communicate them so that they can use them as fuel for change in their personal lives. In this case, emotional ventilation is like drilling for oil in order to use it to mobilize society. To drill for oil simply for the sake of drilling for oil is useless.

The following are examples of unhelpful ventilation:

- A person ventilates emotions for the sole purpose of feeling relief. This person saves up feelings that should have been expressed at the time they were felt. Periodically, the person regurgitates them and feels better, only to return again to saving up feelings that should be expressed if the person is to grow.
- A person ventilates feelings with the wrong person, rather than with the person who is the target of the feelings. For example, as long as a man ventilates regularly with a minister, he never has to communicate feelings with his wife. This deprives the marriage of a critical source of growth.
- A person ventilates feelings that are caused by a misperception. For example, a woman falsely believes that her husband is having an affair. She presents her belief to the minister as fact and dissolves into a deluge of emotions. The more she ventilates and the more she incurs the minister's support, the more she is reinfecting herself with inappropriate emotions and entrenching her false belief.
- A person ventilates feelings as a form of manipulation. A man may "completely open up" with a minister, at least subconsciously hoping that as a result the minister will get him a job or intercede for him in an argument with his wife or with a court of law.
- A person ventilates feelings as a style of relating. Some people relate through emotional ventilation because it forces others to get involved with them. This style creates a one-way communication in which the ventilator receives all the concern and is expected to give none. It also keeps other people off balance and unable to confront the ventilator with his or her contribution to the problem.

Ministers need to be aware that emotional ventilation, like surgery, should be done selectively, intelligently, and probably less frequently than it is done. A minister's ritual-like response, "And how do you feel about this?" often should be replaced with, "Now, let's go back and make sure you're seeing the situation accurately," or "What are you planning to do about this upsetting situation?" or "Why do you think sharing this emotion will help you more now than it seemed to help the last time we talked?"

MYTH V: ALL RELIGIOUS PROBLEMS HAVE RELIGIOUS SOLUTIONS

There are seven areas in which people can experience difficulties: physical, intellectual, emotional, social, sexual, moral, and religious. A problem in one area can be referred to another, just as a pain in one part of the body (e.g., the heart) can be referred to another (e.g., the left arm). A physician would be foolish, however, to treat the sore left arm of a patient who is, in fact, in the midst of a heart attack.

By the same principle, a person may present a problem that seems religious in nature, but the basic problem may stem from one or more of the other six areas of personality. For example, a twenty-year-old woman may be overweight (physical); which causes her to perceive herself as ugly (intellectual); which causes her to feel loathsome toward herself (emotional); which causes her not to date (social); which leads her to masturbate (sexual); which causes her to feel great guilt (moral); which causes her to believe that God has rejected her (religious). This woman seeks the help of a minister because she feels alienated from God.

Simply assuring the woman that God loves her unconditionally, or attempting to help her stop her sexual behavior, or advising her that she need not feel guilty about her sexual behavior will not help her. Ministers must have a holistic view that recognizes that people are multidimensional and their problems are multi-determined. While no one can be an expert at dealing with all seven dimensions of behavior, ministers can deal with the areas in which they feel competent and make appropriate referrals to other helpers so that the person can receive complete attention.

MYTH VI: PEOPLE ARE RELIABLE EYEWITNESSES

Sometimes people are expert eyewitnesses to reality, but mostly they are not, especially when they are emotionally involved in a situation. People can perceive reality through three kinds of perceptual lenses: a clear lens, which renders an accurate view of reality; a positive lens, which makes reality look better than it is; or a negative lens, which makes reality look worse than it is. To complicate matters, the same person can use a different lens with different areas of his or her life.

A woman may view her relationship with her minister with a clear lens, her husband and children with a positive lens, and herself with a negative lens. The minister sees that she is perceiving their relationship accurately; hence, the minister is led to believe the woman perceives all of reality accurately.

However, ministers are not always at the mercy of a person's perceptions. They can avail themselvs of four safeguards. First, whenever possible they should ask to see the other people who are involved in the problem (spouses, parents, children). Ministers frequently will be surprised to see that the devils and the angels they expected to see do not materialize.

Secondly, ministers should be continually aware of the possibility of tinted and distorted perceptions and seek to get a balanced picture by asking questions such as "Jim, you say your wife nags you all the time. If she were sitting in that empty chair listening to us, what would she respond?" or "Nancy, you say that Bob is losing interest in you. What exactly do you see that makes you believe that?" The answers to these questions can give the minister some important information and bring him or her closer to the reality of the situation.

Thirdly, the accuracy of a person's perceptions can often (though not always) be tested in a helping relationship. For example, when ministers find themselves being perceived through positive or negative lenses, or realize that they have an entirely different view of what was said in a previous visit, they can begin at least to build a hypothesis about the accuracy of the person's perceptions.

Finally, when it becomes clear that a person is skewing perceptions in one direction or another, the minister can point this out and help the person realize that many problems stem not from reality but from the fact that the person has a vested interest in seeing reality as better or worse than it actually is.

MYTH VII: PEOPLE WHO SEEK HELP REALLY WANT HELP

Some people who seek help genuinely want it, but others seek help for reasons that are not associated with growth or making situations better. In fact, people may use a minister in ways that reinforce their problems. The following are some common nontherapeutic reasons that motivate people to make an appointment with a minister. Some individuals may wish to see a minister in order

- to get someone "off their back": Parents, a spouse, or friends may have put pressure on a person to get help, even though the person does not want it. The person's real motive is to return to the referral person and report that he or she has visited a minister, and it did not do any good.

- to gather support for their position: A man resents the fact that his wife has taken a job. He tells a minister about the many "problems" his family is having since his wife went to work. The man hopes that the minister will diagnose the family's "problems" as caused by the wife's return to work. If the man is successful, he can return to his wife with an "edict from God" that she should quit her job.

- to get the minister to make a decision for them: A young woman wants to break off her engagement but lacks the courage to do so. She paints a bleak picture of her relationship with her fiance and hopes to lead the minister into suggesting that she at least should postpone the wedding if not break off the relationship. This way, she does not have to take full responsibility for her behavior and can blame the minister if things do not turn out right.

- to have the minister work a miracle: A man hates his job, has not loved his wife for ten years, regrets having children, has no friends or interests, and does not want to get professional

counseling. But he does want to feel a lot better about himself
and life. In other words, like many people, he wants to feel
better without getting better.   *E · Berne must want to Feel better but not change*

- to have someone to talk to who is safe and who has to listen: A
  woman who does not like people, including the significant
  others in her life, regularly visits a minister, mostly to complain
  about life. As long as she has this "support," she can live out
  the rest of her life disliking and avoiding people.

- to get into a special relationship with the minister: A woman
  admires a minister and believes that if she could become his
  close friend, this would enhance her reputation, both in her
  own eyes and those of others.

- to be declared hopeless: A man tells a minister how dreadful
  both he and his life are and deflects all the minister's attempts
  to inject some hope into the situation. The man's motive is to
  be pronounced psychologically dead so that he can avoid the
  stress of trying to better himself and his life.

- to remain victims while deluding themselves and others that
  they are trying to make things better: A woman feels victim-
  ized in a marriage, and although she approaches a minister for
  help, she wishes, at least subconsciously, to remain a victim
  because vicitms have certain rights. These rights include the
  right to complain without taking steps to remedy the situation
  or to confront it directly and the right to receive sympathy and
  financial support while maintaining freedom from
  responsibility.

It is important for ministers to be aware of the various motives
people have for seeking help. This does not mean that people
with countertherapeutic motives should be rejected; however, it
does mean that the countertherapeutic motives must be confronted and the person given the opportunity to change his or
her motives to helpful ones. For ministers to continue to see people whose motives are contrary to the goals of a helping relationship is not only unhelpful but damaging.

PITFALLS MINISTERS ENCOUNTER

Ministers can do a great deal of good for people. Unfortunately, however, they can also do a great deal of harm, as can anyone who deals with intimate and important issues. Therefore, it is helpful to recognize some of the pitfalls that ministers can fall into without being aware of what is happening. The following pitfalls can cause a minister's efforts to be impeded and, at times, to be psychologically and spiritually damaging.

BECOMING A MANAGER

It is often tempting to want to take over for a person who seems to be floundering and helpless. It is easier for a minister to take the approach, "Here, let me tell you what to do next," or "Here, let me mold you into the kind of person you should be," than to go through the slower and more arduous process of helping the person become his or her own architect, gradually drawing the blueprints that will make him or her more effective and fulfilled.

Just as the process of solving a math problem is as important as the answer, so is it important for people to go through the process of becoming more self-directing. When ministers give people answers simply because it is easier to do so, the people are deprived of learning the processes and must always return for answers to future problems.

BECOMING AN AGENT

A minister can be induced into becoming an agent, ambassador, and interceder for the person who seeks the minister's help. Although it could be appropriate to be an agent in a specific circumstance, in the vast majority of cases it is not. People sometimes want ministers to intercede for them with parents, spouses, teachers, employers, or the court. Intercede, as it is used here, means to appeal to a third party in an effort to allow the person to escape the consequences of his or her behavior and/or to seduce a third party away from assuming a position that is appropriate. For example, a minister may be asked by a man to speak to his wife so that she will take him back, even though her decision to separate was well thought out and apparently appropriate. Parents of a student may ask a minister to speak with the principal of a school in order to have a suspension or expulsion rescinded. A woman may ask a minister to intercede with a judge in order to rescue her from the legal and just consequences of her behavior.

When ministers allow themselves to be used as agents in this manner, they are often being exploited in ways that are not ultimately helpful to themselves or to the people involved. It seems more appropriate and constructive to help people handle their difficulties and learn from them. Doing so makes them less likely to find themselves in similar situations in the future.

ASSUMING A ROLE OTHER THAN THAT OF MINISTER

A minister in a helping relationship must remember that he or she is a minister, not a friend, a father, a mother, a husband, a wife, or a lover. There is an important difference between caring about a person as a good friend would, or as a parent or a spouse would, and assuming the role of a friend, a parent, a spouse, or a lover. When a minister assumes one or more of these roles, he or she is violating reality, because, in fact, the minister is not a social friend, a parent, a spouse, or a lover of the person.

Ministers must be able to remain *within* the ministerial role:

- to remain objective and not become emotionally caught up in the perceptions and moods of the person;
- to care enough to be helpful, but not so much as to become overinvested or overprotective;
- to allow the person the freedom to follow his or her own lights, even when this process may involve making some mistakes;
- to be free to be absolutely honest without an inordinate fear of "losing" the person;
- to remain steadfast against the manipulation, needs, and values of the person that are inappraite and/or unhelpful.

While the ideal friend, spouse, or parent should possess all of these abilities, in reality emotional attachment often diminishes one's ability to be truly helpful.

ADHERING TO ONE THEORY

It is hoped that ministers will familiarize themselves with the ideas of respected psychologists and theologians in an effort to become more effective in helping people. However, ministers must be aware of the temptation to find a theorist with whom they agree and feel comfortable and to use the teachings of that theorist with every person in every situation as if the theory were a master key.

Twenty years ago Carl Rogers was in vogue in ministry, possibly because listening, empathizing, accepting, and clarifying did not appear to call for many skills. After Rogers, Eric Berne became fashionable in ministry, possibly because his basic concepts were simple to grasp and appeared simple to use. Currently Carl Jung seems to be popular in ministry, possibly because he deals with the religious-spiritual dimension of human beings more explicitly than some other theorists.

However, objectivity demands a closer look at any theorist along several lines. First, although each of the above theorists has something of importance to teach, they all also have their serious limitations. Yet it seems that ministers are often far more conversant with what they like about each theorist and far less knowledgeable and cautious about the serious limitations of each. Second, these theories are far more complex and complicated than most of the people who try to put them into practice seem to realize. Third, when ministers (or any other helpers) closely identify with a specific theory, they are more likely to stretch people to fit the theory than to find theories to fit the people. Finally, when ministers appeal to one theory, they are inclined to use the theorist as a third person in the helping relationship, which serves to distract from the relationship and dilute it. For example, if the minister sees herself as a Jungian, there may be three important people in the counseling relationship: the person seeking help, the minister, and Jung, whose presence may overshadow the person and the minister. While the minister may be saying, "Well, Jung addresses this problem when he says . . . ," the person seeking help may well be saying to himself, "Who cares what Jung thinks? I only care what you and I think."

The more ministers can develop an appreciation for the ideas of several psychologists and theologians, the more keys they will have to open more doors for a wider range of people. However, the effectiveness of a key is completely contingent on the person who is using it.

OVERESTIMATING ONE'S POWER

When people approach a minister for help they usually have tried to solve the problem themselves and have procrastinated about seeking outside help. Moreover, ministers by nature want to help people in general and especially those who have specifically sought their help. The combination of a pressing problem and a strong need to be helpful can create a destructive force which causes the minister to act prematurely without exercising sufficient patience, prudence, or wisdom.

For the most part, the problems that people bring to ministers have been present, or at least incubating, for some time. Therefore, it is unlikely that a minister will be able to rush in and fix the situation in one, two, or three visits.

It is also helpful to keep in mind that only the people who created the problem or allowed themselves to become part of a problem can solve the problem. A minister cannot swoop into a difficult situation, make a few declarations, and expect the situation to be rehabilitated. A problem can be solved only to the extent that (1) the problem is solvable; (2) the people involved have the competence to solve it; (3) the people involved have a deep desire to solve it. Ministers cannot make an unsolvable problem solvable. Ministers may be able to do something about helping a person increase his or her competencies to solve the problem or to increase a person's desire to solve the problem. As used here, the word *may* means *maybe*, depending on many variables, and the word *something* connotes the midpoint between nothing and everything.

When ministers understand the ways in which their powers to help are limited, they are more likely to accept and work within these limits and to harbor realistic expectations of themselves and others. They then will be able to clarify the minister's role for the people involved. In turn, the people can then decide whether or not to pursue further help from the minister. In this way, the minister will get caught up neither in the pressure to effect a miracle, nor in personal desires to be a savior.

In many situations, the most a minister (or any helper) can do is to act as a beacon, shining a light into areas of darkness and encouraging people to explore those areas for solutions. To expect more than this will lead to mutual frustration and disappointment.

YIELDING TO OUTSIDE PRESSURE

It is important that ministers remain free agents; that is, that they do what they think is best for the person they are helping, whether or not others happen to agree.

Often people are referred to ministers by people who have specific ideas as to how they want the person's behavior to change. In other words, they attempt to use the minister as an enforcer and reinforcer of their own wishes and values. For example, parents may view their teenage son's healthy assertive behavior as "disruptive" and want the minister to show the boy the importance of respect.

Whenever a person approaches a minister for help at the request or demand of another, the minister must take care to understand the exact nature of the situation. Many times, people are referred to ministers not for the purpose of increasing their psychological and spiritual health, but to be shaped in ways that please the referral source.

When the expectation of the referral source clashes with sound principles of psychological and spiritual health, the minister is caught in a bind. If the minister follows the prescription of the referral source, he or she will be doing a gross injustice to the person who is there to be helped. If the minister judges that the person is behaving in normal and appropriate ways, then the referral source will be upset and behave accordingly.

For this reason, it is of the utmost importance to communicate early to the referral source that the minister must act as a free agent, responding to the situation as he or she deems most in keeping with sound psychological and spiritual values. When ministers feel under pressure to please referral sources, they place themselves in precarious positions because they often may be attempting to be successful in two mutually exclusive endeavors.

SUPPORTING BEHAVIOR THAT SHOULD NOT BE SUPPORTED

Although support and affirmation have their place in helping relationships, they should not be offered reflexively or promiscuously. Even though ministers can attempt to understand all behavior, not all behavior should be supported.

Many people present both themselves and their problems in ways that instantly elicit sympathy and support. They create a tug in the minister that causes him or her to think, "Oh, this poor person! I must help him get what he wants." Before launching a supportive campaign, however, the minister would be well-advised to gather more knowledge and give the issue further consideration.

For example, a nineteen-year-old tells a minister he wants to move away from home and live with a friend. He explains that he wants to become independent and work for a year so he can go to college. He says that he is willing to support himself so that he would not be a burden to his parents. He explains that the only obstacle is his mother, who is overprotective of him, since he is the last child to leave home. He says that it is all right with his father if he leaves.

The young man is nice looking, polite, intelligent, and concerned that he will hurt his mother if he leaves. The minister likes the young man and reflects back on how important it was for him to leave home at about the same age, even though his mother fretted about it.

The minister's "supportive button" has been successfully pushed, and he assures the young man that all mothers feel the same when their youngest leaves home and that she will soon adapt to it. However, the minister is unaware of a number of mitigating circumstances.

First, the young man is struggling with a drug problem and plans to move in with a friend who uses drugs. The young man's mother suspects this and feels her son still needs some adult support and supervision at home before he is strong enough to place himself in that situation. Although the young man says he wants to pay his own way, he has no money or job prospects. His idea of paying his own way is to ask for a loan from his parents which he promises to repay "as soon as I can." In the midst of a heated discussion with his parents, the young man's father said, "Well, if that's the way you think, maybe it would be better if you moved out." The young man takes this statement out of context and uses it as an indication that his father agrees with the decision to move away.

In this example, the well-intentioned, but naive, minister views himself (herself) as helping a young man fly from the nest and take an important first step toward adulthood. If the minister had been more objective and asked some "impolite" but important questions, and especially if he had spoken with both the parents and the son together, the minister would have taken a different and potentially more helpful approach.

DEALING WITH SOMEONE ALREADY IN COUNSELING

Sometimes a person who is seeing a professional counselor or therapist will also seek the help of a minister. This can often be a precarious situation for at least three reasons.

First, the counselor may be trying to help the person through a particularly sensitive part of counseling. Like a surgeon doing microscopic surgery, the counselor is attempting to get at a psychological "tumor," which necessitates great delicacy, precision, and balance. It would not be unusual for a person going through this process to consult a minister whom he or she knows and trusts.

A problem arises, however, if the minister is unaware of the intricacies of the situation and jumps into the middle of the microscopic surgery already in progress. For example, a counselor may have worked long and hard helping a man accept responsibility for his marital problems. As the man comes closer to this important insight, he becomes more anxious and goes to a minister with at least the subconscious purpose of having the minister's reassurance that he is a helpless victim rather than a co-conspirator in the marital problems.

The unsuspecting minister tries to be affirming and supportive and assures the man that he is a better person than the counselor is giving him credit for and makes a comment about professional counselors being "too negative" at times. Instead of being helpful, this session with the minister cost the man twenty hours of counseling and probably a great deal of hard-earned money. Moreover, it possibly placed the man's relationship with his counselor in jeopardy.

A second, related problem can arise when a minister deals with a person already in counseling. The person may be going through a difficult stage in the counseling process and may be looking subconsciously for an excuse to terminate counseling prematurely. For example, a woman may make an appointment with her minister and relate incidents which "clearly" show the counselor to be inept, if not incompetent; peculiar, if not disturbed; and amoral, if not immoral. The minister predictably and on cue reacts with concern, suggesting that the woman discontinue counseling and either see her or another counselor. This kind of situation presents another example of how important it is to consult with a person's primary counselor before becoming involved in the situation.

A third problem arises when a person has two helpers: a counselor and a minister. Sometimes this combination can work well if both helpers keep in touch with each other, especially during difficult times. However, the combination is not likely to be helpful if the two helpers do not communicate, and even then the chances are not especially good that the combination will be helpful to the person. The reason for this is that when two helpers—regardless of their professions—are working with the same person (or couple), the "too many chefs spoil the broth" syndrome is as likely to occur as not. Unlike surgery, where there are only a few standardized ways to perform a particular operation, there are many ways to go about helping a person with a problem.

For example, two helpers may be working with a man who is depressed. One helper, because of the nature of his education, experience, personality, and unique relationship with the person, may want to focus on the man's pent-up hostility, which is a major cause of the depression. His immediate goal is to help the man learn to express his anger in constructive ways. The other helper, because of her education, experience, personality, and unique relationship with the man, chooses to focus on his loneliness, which is also a major cause of his depression. The net result is that the man spends half his time trying to bring new people into his life (to decrease his loneliness) and half his time expressing anger at these new people (to decrease his hostility). The man soon finds that he is working at cross-purposes.

Both helpers are competent, but they are working against each other, and the man is caught in the middle. Depending upon the specific nature of the man's problem, it might be better for him to work on the anger first and the loneliness second, or vice versa. But to work on both at the same time could be a frustrating and fruitless pursuit.

In summary, it is not only helpful but very important to recognize and understand some of the basic principles and pitfalls in pastorally helping people. Sometimes ministers delude themselves into thinking that their intelligence, sensitivity, and experience are sufficient grounds for embarking on a counseling relationship with a person. What should be kept in mind is that there is little correlation between intelligence and being psychological-ly minded, between sensitivity and being psychologically at-tuned, and between unsupervised and supervised experience.

CAUTIONS IN PASTORAL COUNSELING

As we have seen, dealing with the psychological dimension of human behavior is very complex. Dealing with the spiritual di-mension is also very complex. Evaluating, treating, and healing them together is *infinitely* complex. In addition to the complexity of pastoral counseling, there is the potential to do great good or great harm, even in one counseling session.

We have also seen that it is both ironic and frightening how some of the same people who would never dream of treating the body are dauntless when it comes to treating people's psyches and souls. Pastoral counselors who are apt to be the most effec-tive are those who know what to be cautious about and how to act accordingly. The following section is included to review and expand upon some of the areas of caution of which ministers in general, and pastoral counselors in particular, should be aware.

BE CLEAR ABOUT THE PASTORAL COUNSELOR'S ROLE

It is important that pastoral counselors have a clear definition of their role so that they do not slide into roles that are at best un-helpful, and at worst harmful. Just as it is vitally important that surgeons function as surgeons and not as psychiatrists, it is es-sential that pastoral counselors function as such and not as other types of counselors or ministers. For example, pastoral counsel-ors, when they function as pastoral counselors, are not regular counselors, general pastoral ministers, or spiritual directors.

Regular counselors spend several years of postgraduate educa-tion and training before they are eligible for state licensing. Although they are ordinarily more competent than pastoral counselors to deal with psychosocial problems that are in the diagnosable range, they do not have training in pastoral issues.

General pastoral care ministers help people meet their daily physical, psychosocial, and spiritual needs. General pastoral care is typically more directive, educational, and short-term, as well as less structured, clinical, and confrontive than pastoral counseling.

Spiritual directors help people deepen their union with God by increasing their awareness of God's presence in themselves, others, and the world at large. Spiritual directors help people seek answers to questions such as "Who is the Lord to me?" and "Who am I to the Lord?"

Pastoral counselors have specific education and training in the area of pastoral counseling. Their competence lies in helping people with concerns or problems that have *both* psychosocial *and* moral-religious implications.

Relative to their proper role and area of competence, ministers in general, and pastoral counselors in particular, must recognize, first of all, that they should offer people what they ask for and what they need. If people seek pastoral counseling, they should not be offered regular counseling. Pastoral counseling was never meant to be a substitute for regular counseling or a way to avoid whatever stigma is still attached to seeing a regular counselor or psychotherapist. Ministers will see this point more clearly if they consider the possibility of people who need pastoral counseling going to regular counselors because they do not feel comfortable with ministers.

By the same professional and ethical principles, people who ask for and need pastoral counseling should not be offered general pastoral care, spiritual direction, religious education, or evangelization. Nor should people who need general pastoral care or spiritual direction be given pastoral counseling.

Secondly, as we have seen earlier, ministers must recognize that what people *ask for* and what they *need* may not be the same. A person may seek help from a pastoral counselor, but after evaluation, it may become clear that he actually needs regular counseling; another person may think she needs pastoral counseling when, in fact, she needs spiritual direction; yet another may think he needs spiritual direction when he actually needs pastoral counseling.

Finally, ministers must realize that although there is some minimal overlap between most, if not all, subspecialties of ministry, they are essentially quite separate, and require specific education, training, and competence. Therefore, like any professional, the minister can intelligently and comfortably refer people to the appropriate minister or counselor and not attempt to help people who require a service that falls outside his or her area of competence.

RECOGNIZE THE PROBLEM'S COMPLEXITY

Pastoral counselors can be faced with relatively simple to very complex situations, and it is important that they recognize the difference.

One area of complexity lies in distinguishing between a person's *stated* problem and his or her *real* problem or problems. It is not uncommon that a person's stated problem is not his real problem because the person is unaware of what the real problem is or is reluctant to discuss it. Moreover, when people are experiencing so much distress that they must seek help from a counselor, they often have more than one problem.

For example, a woman may tell a pastoral counselor that her problem is that she is falling out of love with her husband and in love with another man. It could be that her stated problem is her real one. However, the chances are easily as good that it is not.

It could be that her real problem is that her need to control the people and events that are important to her is causing her husband to withdraw, either by spending more time at work or by becoming depressed and, therefore, "lazy and boring." The less love she feels from her husband, the more she tries to control him, which pushes him further into his work or deeper into his depression. Eventually, she finds a man who, for whatever reasons, shows her some affection, and she falls in love with him. Sooner or later, as her need for this man increases, so will her need to control him, thus beginning the whole cycle once again.

The pastoral counselor who focuses either on getting the woman's husband to be more attentive or on helping the woman leave her husband will seriously miss the target. The pastoral counselor who, gradually and judiciously, helps the woman realize that her need to control is causing her to lose what she wants the most, namely, the love of people she loves, will at least present an opportunity for the woman to save both herself and her marriage. It may be that the minister will have to work with the couple, and not just the woman, to resolve the problem successfully.

It could also be that the woman controls her husband because he behaves more like a child than an adult, and the only way to hold the family together is to manage him. However, her husband may resent the fact that she manages him and withdraws in order to escape her control. In other words, the husband is placing his wife in a double bind: if she doesn't manage him, he participates in irresponsible behavior; when she does manage him, he uses this as an excuse to withdraw. So, the woman becomes tired of her husband's withdrawal and finds another man.

In this case, the woman actually has three problems. First, she has a husband who is psychosocially stunted and will need some concentrated help. Second, she has fallen into a trap by agreeing to manage her husband, which makes her a contributing cause of the problem. Third, she *thinks* she is falling in love with another man, but what she is calling "love" is actually a mixture of three powerful feelings: affirmation ("See, I *am* attractive, despite what my husband thinks"), fear ("I *must* feel love for him or he may stop loving me"), and guilt ("As long as I *love* him and am not just using him, our relationship is all right").

The pastoral counselor who focuses on any one or two of the problems will miss the target. It is the subtle and intricate interaction of all three problems that must be unraveled and addressed by both the woman and her husband.

Even from these brief examples, it can be seen that problems will arise when pastoral counselors automatically assume that stated problems are real ones, or that stated problems are the only problems present.

Another area of complexity lies in *distinguishing between prob-*

lems and symptoms. Typically, people refer to their symptoms as their problems. For example, a man tells a pastoral counselor that his problem is that he is depressed when, in fact, his *symptom* is depression, but his *problem* is either that he is repressing strong feelings of loneliness, resentment, or guilt, or that he has an endocrine dysfunction. To treat this man's symptom (depression) directly by encouraging him to reduce his work load, get more sleep and exercise, appreciate his blessings, see the bright side of life, or pray more will only increase his depression because none of these homespun remedies will work.

A third area of complexity lies in the area of cause-and-effect relationships. Grave problems arise when specious cause-and-effect relationships are postulated and acted upon. For example, a husband complains to a pastoral counselor, "My wife was the best wife and mother in the world until she hit forty-five. Then she completely changed. She's going through a mid-life crisis, but she's not pulling out of it." If the pastoral counselor accepts the husband's reported cause-and-effect relationship (problematic behavior caused by mid-life crisis), the counselor will make a serious mistake. In reality, the man's wife has never been as psychologically and spiritually healthy. The behavior that is upsetting the husband is that his wife has finally grown sufficiently in psychological strength to stand up to his dominating and manipulative behavior. Moreover, she is finishing college, meeting new friends, and pursuing other healthy interests that she has deprived herself of because of her husband's possessiveness and jealousy. The pastoral counselor who perceives the true cause-and-effect situation (wife's psychosocial growth creates significant anxiety in her husband because he feels he will lose control over her or lose her to someone else) will be able to construct an appropriate counseling plan, whether or not the husband is willing to participate in it.

Distinguishing between stated causes and real causes, symptoms and problems, and specious and true cause-and-effect relationships are only three of a myriad of complexities inherent in pastoral counseling.

REALIZE THAT PEOPLE ARE UNIQUE

Pastoral counselors should be exquisitely aware of how different each individual is and how much harm can result from assuming similarities that don't exist.

There are at least three basic mistakes that pastoral counselors can make in this area. The first is to have a set of "therapeutic shoulds" that they accept as universally valid and apply to the people with whom they work in their ministry. The following are a few examples of some common "therapeutic shoulds" that are as likely to create problems as they are to reduce them:

- People who are having problems should get counseling (even when they possess none of the qualities necessary to benefit from it, for example, at least an adequate degree of motivation, openness, insight).
- People who are having problems should get in touch with their spiritual side and renew their relationship with God (even when the moral inventory required to do this would create an intolerable degree of guilt and self-loathing at this point).
- People who are having problems should become less selfish and more sensitive to the needs and feelings of others (even when it is exactly this combination that has created the majority of their problems in the first place).
- Married couples who are having problems should sit down with each other, with or without a counselor, and discuss their honest feelings in order to clear the air (even when the people are not even close to being ready to acknowledge those feelings to themselves, much less to acknowledge them to the other or to hear them from each other).
- Childless married couples who are having problems should have children to get their minds off themselves (even when they cannot handle the domestic stress they already have).

A second mistake pastoral counselors make regarding different people's individuality is to assume that what helped one person with a particular problem will help another person with a similar problem. For example, a pastoral counselor has suggested to parents who were grieving over the death of their child that they go away together for a few days and strengthen their love and support for each other. Because this suggestion seemed to be helpful in the past, the counselor makes the same recommendation to another set of grieving parents. The second couple take her advice, but spend the days away blaming each other for the child's death.

A third mistake is to operate on the "If I were you . . . " principle. For example, a pastoral counselor advising a troubled seminarian may think or even say, "If I were you, I would take a leave of absence from the seminary, get some counseling, engage in dating, and find a job. Then I would reassess matters a year from now." There is a big problem with this approach: the pastoral counselor is *not* the seminarian, never was the seminarian, and never will be the seminarian. In cases like this, pastoral counselors may be saying more about their own needs than addressing themselves to the needs of the other.

All of these mistakes stem from the failure to realize intellectually and emotionally that each individual is comprised of a unique combination of genes, constitution, and learning. Pastoral counselors must treat individuals as if they are unique because, in fact, they are. To foist pseudo-universals on people, whether the universals come from the Church, society, or one's own private notions, is to invite significant problems in pastoral counseling.

BE REALISTIC ABOUT HUMAN BEHAVIOR

It is important that pastoral counselors have a realistic view of human behavior so that they do not fall into traps that are mutually damaging.

Being realistic about human behavior lies midpoint between being naive (optimistic) and suspicious (pessimistic). Great harm can result when pastoral counselors lean toward either end of this range. When Christians err in this regard, they tend to do so on the naive side.

To be realistic and to avoid harmful naivete, it is important, first of all, for pastoral counselors to distinguish between helping people *feel* better and helping them *get* better. Many, if not most, distressed people who seek help from pastoral counselors want to be told that their distress is not their responsibility but that of their spouse, child, parent, friend, boss, or religious superior; or that they are partially responsible for their distress, but someone else is far more responsible for it; or that what others are perceiving as problematic behavior in them is really appropriate, if not actually healthy, behavior; or that they cannot feel better until a significant other changes the way he or she behaves toward them; or, finally, that the Church, Scripture, and God are on their side and not on the side of whoever seems to be the source of their distress.

Obviously, if any one of these assurances is appropriate to the particular counselee's situation, it should be given in one form or another. However, it is likely that in the majority of instances, none of these assurances is appropriate or at least sufficient to help people solve their problems. Therefore, for a pastoral counselor to offer these assurances routinely is to render a disservice, even though people may be temporarily grateful.

Secondly, to be realistic, it is important for pastoral counselors to understand that psycho-religious problems can be mild, moderate, or severe, and that moderate and severe problems may take one, two, or more years of counseling to reduce or resolve significantly. When this is not clearly understood, inappropriate pressure is placed on the person in counseling, as well as on the pastoral counselor, to perform better.

Thirdly, the realistic pastoral counselor should recognize that some people who seek the help of a pastoral counselor do not want to rid themselves of their distress. Consciously or unconsciously, they need to be depressed, anxious, confused, resentful, defensive, hostile, insensitive, uncaring, controlling, obnoxious, suspicious, manipulative, or hedonistic. Such individuals need to hang on to their maladjustive behavior because it gives them some sense of control over their lives and/or the lives of others. For example, as long as a man is depressed, he doesn't have to face what for him are the overpowering anxieties of work, marriage, parenthood, and life in general. If he were to lose his shield of depression, he feels that he would disintegrate in the face of the above-mentioned anxieties. As paradoxical as it may sound, depression is the glue holding the man's psyche and soul together. Anyone, including a pastoral counselor, who seeks to loosen the man's grip on his maladaptive behavior will meet with massive resistance. Sooner or later, the pastoral counselor must face this sort of individual with the true nature and purpose of his symptoms if any progress is to be made.

REALIZE WHAT "PASTORAL" COUNSELING MEANS

It is important that pastoral counselors possess a clear and deep appreciation of what "pastoral" means so that they will be true Christian ministers and not simply regular counselors or, what is worse, damaging counselors.

The term *pastoral* describes behaviors that are both religious (i.e., clearly Christian, Jewish, Moslem, etc.) and helpful (i.e., psychologically sound, theologically enlightened, and humanly empathetic). Counseling that is nonreligious or only superficially religious is not pastoral counseling, and counseling that is religious but not helpful is neither pastoral nor counseling. With this in mind, Christian pastoral counselors should remember these final four recommendations.

First, there is more than one Christian theology; the mainstream of theological thought has many currents. For a minister to have one theology to apply to all people and all situations is analogous to a regular counselor operating from one theory of personality and trying to stretch and shrink everyone's psyche to fit it.

Second, whatever a pastoral counselor's theologies are, they should be clear, articulable, and consistent. Effective pastoral counselors have woven into one thematic fabric their understanding of the nature of God, Scripture, revelation, tradition, grace, morality, Church teachings, authority, and law. This is in contrast to *ad hoc* theologies that lack substance and consistency. For example, a man, grief stricken over the death of his wife, seeks help. The pastoral counselor, reaching instinctively for his box of theological Band-Aids, assures the man that he and his wife will soon be united again in heaven. The man gets a confused look on his face and responds, "But Sunday's gospel reading said that husbands and wives will not be joined together in heaven." Now what does the pastoral counselor do?

Third, it can be helpful for pastoral counselors to realize that part of a well-thought-out theology is the presence and acknowledgment of areas of confusion and ignorance. A pastoral counselor who conveys the impression that he or she possesses all the theological answers also conveys the impression that he or she is ignorant, simple, or arrogant. Part of being pastoral is to share people's ignorance and confusion and its attendant anxieties. This can be far more helpful than scampering about for superficial or nonexistent answers.

Finally, it is important to understand that many of the problems that people bring to pastoral counselors deal directly or indirectly with the Church's teachings on morality. Therefore, it is incumbent on pastoral counselors to have an updated and sound understanding of moral theology. In this regard, the following points can be kept in mind and studied more fully.

- While pastoral counselors must deal with concepts of moral theology, they must also consider the subjective culpability, responsibility, and potential of each individual to act in ways that are more virtuous. In other words, there are agreed-upon differences between the moral order and the pastoral order.

- When a person faces a dilemma in which he or she cannot avoid any evil no matter what is done, traditional wisdom requires the individual to pursue the greater duty.

- People may not be psycho-spiritually capable of changing their behavior overnight. Thus, they should be judged and judge themselves according to their attempts as well as the results of their efforts.

- The principle of fundamental option means looking at the person's fundamental or basic life theme when evaluating the gravity of specific acts. For example, a person who generally lives a life of Christian love and justice would be judged less harshly for isolated immoral acts than would a person who chooses to live a life of selfishness and exploitation.

• The moral law and a moral decision are not the same. Moral law consists of objective and universal principles, whereas a moral decision results from an intellectual, affective, and spiritual discernment as to whether the law serves to increase or decrease the gospel virtues of love, justice, and freedom in an individual's life and/or relationships. The process of making a personal moral decision consists of knowing and respecting the formal teachings of the Church, the *praxis* of believers in the community, the work of theologians, the sense and experience of all Christians, dialogue with a representative of the Church, and prayerful discernment. In the last analysis, it is the individual who must make and assume responsibility for his or her decision.

In summary, the practice of pastoral counseling, like regular counseling, can be helpful, unhelpful, or harmful. Unfortunately, the harmful psychological and spiritual effects are not as readily visible as comparable effects on the body. Therefore, ministers must develop an acute sensitivity to what can harm the psyches and souls of people in counseling.

This ability stems from both a natural sensitivity and a cultivated sensitivity that can be acquired by regularly reading relevant material, attending courses, seminars, and workshops, as well as acquiring as much supervised counseling experience as possible. Finally, especially with difficult counseling situations, it is important for pastoral ministers (counselors) to be able to discuss the issue with another counselor in order to deepen and broaden their vision.

Pastoral counseling is not for amateurs or for people who are professionals in related but different fields. Pastoral counseling is a serious endeavor, as serious as the practice of medicine or law, and some would even say that the stakes are infinitely higher.

3. Helps and Hindrances in Ministry

As is true with any endeavor, there are behaviors that help a minister to reach and touch people in ways that matter. Other behaviors, however, cause ministers to undershoot or overshoot the mark. This chapter will discuss five areas that, depending upon how they are handled, will increase or diminish the effectiveness of a minister.

"SELVES" THAT HELP OR HINDER MINISTRY

The relationship between the self of the minister and effective communication lies in the fact that the self is the vehicle by which the minister conveys the teachings of Jesus to others. When the self is healthy, it acts as an effective vehicle; when the self is tainted, it becomes a barrier to Christian communication. It is important to realize that verbal communication is incidental in relation to the self. In other words, wrong words can often be rehabilitated by a healthy self, and right words can often be negated by an unhealthy self. It is possible for a minister to say all the right things but be the wrong person.

There are at least four kinds of self that can operate within a minister: the Ministerial Self, the Narcissistic Self, the Burnt-out Self, and the Healthy Self.

THE MINISTERIAL SELF

Consciously or unconsciously, the Ministerial Self is programmed according to the minister's view of what a minister should be. Ministers who operate largely from the Ministerial Self spend more time *acting* like ministers than being *human beings* who function as ministers. The following are some axioms according to which the Ministerial Self functions:

- Ministers should only feel and communicate ministerial emotions (compassion, happiness, joy, hope, and love) and not feel or communicate other emotions (fear, frustration, loneliness, jealousy, hurt, sadness, anger, helplessness), even when such emotions are appropriate and potentially helpful.
- Ministers should be perfect, or at least very close to perfect. They should have all the answers and do and say all the right things. They should not convey uncertainty, ignorance, confusion, ambivalence, or awkwardness, even when such states are present and/or appropriate.
- Ministers should always have a religious sentiment to offer in a time of crisis, whether or not it flows from the minister's heart or is appropriate or meaningful to the person.
- Ministers should never say no, even when acceding to a request may cause them undue hardship and/or not be in the best interests of the other people involved.
- Ministers should always be nice, even when it would be more appropriate and/or helpful to express disagreement or to confront people regarding inappropriate behavior.
- Ministers should be asexual and treat others as asexual, even though no one is asexual in reality.
- Ministers should assume that everyone who is suffering needs their help and act accordingly, whether or not the people could better cope with the situation by themselves.
- Ministers should teach people what is right and wrong, even though helping people form their own consciences and make their own decisions is a preferable, moral endeavor.

Ministers who operate largely from a Ministerial Self do so either because they have lost touch with their real selves or because they do not like or trust their real selves. The pastoral problem with operating from a Ministerial Self is that ministers come across either as so perfect that people cannot identify with them, or so artificial that people do not trust them, or so intrusive as to be abrasive. The personal problem with operating from a Ministerial Self is that the minister's true self suffocates under the mantle of ministry, causing subliminal, if not conscious, feelings of confusion, resentment, isolation, anxiety, or depression.

THE NARCISSISTIC SELF

This self is operated by the minister's need to be successful, liked, needed, and admired. Narcissism is a quality rarely discussed with regard to ministry because it is erroneously assumed that apostolic work and narcissism would not exist together. In reality, however, religious work can be both an effective instrument of, and a disguise for, narcissism. The following are some qualities of ministers who function largely according to a Narcissistic Self:

- They tend to overwork because they are working fifty percent for the Lord and seventy-five percent for themselves, which means they are working at least twenty-five percent more than is good for them or their apostolate.
- They focus more on how they are doing in the pastoral relationship than on how the person(s) in the relationship is doing.
- They overreact to frustration and failure because their ego-involvement is greater than their soul-involvement.
- They view other people as rungs on the ladder of their personal success, placing subtle pressure on people to react in ways that will make the minister feel successful.
- They have creative and well-disguised ways of letting their virtues and successes be generally known in order to boost their status.
- They are unduly energized by compliments and inordinately demoralized when their efforts are unnoticed or unaffirmed.
- They approach each new pastoral relationship as a chance to succeed or fail, rather than as an opportunity to bring peace.

Ministers who operate largely from a Narcissistic Self do so because, deep down, they doubt their worth; consequently, each day they must convince themselves and others that they are lovable and capable. The pastoral problem with operating from a Narcissistic Self is that, sooner or later, it becomes clear that what appeared to be ministry was actually manipulation, and this creates a good deal of hurt and disillusionment.

The personal problem with a Narcissistic Self is that genuine self-esteem is largely unrelated to performance or acclaim. Like a person attempting to fill an urn with a hole in the bottom, the narcissistic minister works feverishly each day to become filled with love, only to wake up each morning empty. Hence, the whole process must begin again, *ad infinitum*.

THE BURNT-OUT SELF

This self has been driven too fast and too long without proper physical, psychological, and spiritual lubrication. It still has a few more miles in it, but it runs poorly and is being increasingly damaged each day. A Burnt-out Self is likely to have once been a Ministerial or Narcissistic Self, because Healthy Selves do not have the overdriven needs that cause burnout. The following are some qualities of a minister functioning with a Burnt-out Self:

- Individuals and families who were once viewed as people to heal are now seen as jobs to be gotten out of the way. As one minister said, "I'm sick and tired of working with people who are sick and tired."
- The ring of the phone or the beep of the pager which once signaled an opportunity to be helpful now produces dread and resentment.
- The pastoral team which was once a source of support and enjoyment is now viewed as a further drain on time, energy, and goodwill.
- Days off which were once sources of nourishment are now wasted with meaningless tasks and too much eating, sleeping, drinking, and smoking.
- "Doing for" people has replaced "being with" people. "Who can I *be* for you?" is now replaced with "What can I *do* for you?" because "doing" is less draining and painful than "being."

- Prayer which was once a time of peace, solace, reflection, and recreation has become a burden and has been jettisoned in order to lighten the load of a minister quickly losing altitude.
- Listening has been short-circuited by inner noises; patience has been obliterated by irritability; and compassion has been usurped by self-pity.

Ministers who operate largely from a Burnt-out Self do so because, like a rocket lost in outer space, they cannot stop until they burn out. The general reason for this is that they would not know who they are or what they would do without their work, as unfulfilling as it is.

The pastoral problem with operating from a Burnt-out Self is that other people are ignored, dealt with superficially, or treated poorly. The personal problem is that burnt-out ministers create a vicious circle: the less they treat people well, the more negative feedback they receive; the greater the negative feedback, the more their spirit becomes depleted, causing them to treat people even less well. Some ministers become so burnt-out that they never return to a fully functioning level.

THE HEALTHY SELF

This self has two qualities: it is relatively pure in that it is not contaminated by the other Selves; and it is at least reasonably secure and alive (self-actualized). A Healthy Self is an effective vehicle by which the teachings of Christ can be conveyed, both verbally and nonverbally. The following are some qualities of ministers who operate from a Healthy Self:

- They are authentic; that is, they operate on the principle, "Who you see is who I am." They are willing to share their thoughts, feelings, and imperfections as they arise, which, in turn allows them to be spontaneous and to flow with situations rather than react in ways that are unduly self-conscious or scripted.
- They are sufficiently secure and self-contained, which allows them to focus on the needs of the person rather than on their own needs. This frees them from becoming overextended

("The more people I touch, the better person and minister I am"), overinvolved ("The more deeply involved I become, the more I can feel needed"), and overwrought ("It tears me apart to see people suffer and not be able to do anything about it").

- They possess a realistic sense of themselves and others. They do not expect too much of themselves and others; hence, they avoid becoming dispirited when unrealistic expectations are not met. On the other hand, they are not pessimistic. Therefore, they avoid a "What's the use?" attitude that slackens motivation and creates cynicism.

- They possess a humility that is healthy and realistic. They realize that they will not be able to reach some people, although other ministers might be able to do so. They know that some, perhaps many, people can do quite nicely without their help. They realize that sometimes they can make matters worse. They recognize that they do not like or care about some of the people they have been assigned to help. They freely expect to make at least one mistake each day, and they fully expect to learn from it.

- They are freeing. Like good waiters, they show people the varying menu of spiritual nourishment they have to offer, and then allow people to choose what, if anything, they want. Because they respect both God's will and free will, they do not exert pressure on people to relate to them, to return to the sacraments, to reconcile with others, or to make decisions in a particular direction; nor do they induce guilt in people who chose not to buy their product.

- They take good care of themselves, because they possess a healthy sense of self-respect and self-esteem. They do not overwork, but take adequate time off and use it well. They keep physically fit. They feel free to disappoint people who face them with inappropriate demands and unrealistic expectations. This results in a freshness and buoyancy which energizes them and allows them to be resilient in the face of stress.

- They have a sound sense of spirituality. This means that they keep spiritually alive and centered, due to an ongoing relationship with God. It means that they continue to become educated spiritually so that they can stretch their spirits in the direction of growth and offer people new insights, supports, and challenges. In addition, it means that they have a clear sense of their role as spiritual helpers and do not function merely as half-baked social workers or psychologists.

Ministers with a Healthy Self have grown through and around adversity. This does not mean that they are conflict-free or have reached the peak of psychological and spiritual growth. It simply means that these ministers are significantly more altruistic than selfish, more secure than insecure, more effective than ineffective, all the while realizing that selfishness, insecurity, and ineffectiveness are always present and always need to be addressed.

In summary, since no one has a perfectly Healthy Self, it is likely that ministers can see themselves in two, three, or all four of the Selves described above. Nevertheless it is important for ministers to reflect on what sort of Self they are manifesting. Such reflection can help ministers develop a clearer picture of where they are and where they want to go. Sometimes only slight changes are needed, and these can be accomplished by one's own effort and the help of friends and colleagues. In other instances, professional help is needed to clarify the picture further and to help the minister learn the skills necessary to grow toward a healthier self. In either case, as the Self becomes more pure and healthy, it becomes a more effective and attractive medium of Christian communication.

FACTORS THAT FACILITATE OR INTERFERE WITH EFFECTIVE TEACHING AND PREACHING

Teaching and preaching are basic to ministry, and they mark a second area of behavior that can increase or decrease a minister's effectiveness. Unfortunately, neither teaching nor preaching is done with sufficient élan that people ordinarily look forward to listening to either one. As Anthony Trollope wrote in *Barchester Towers* in 1857, "There is, perhaps, no greater hardship at present

inflicted on mankind in civilised and free countries, than the necessity of listening to sermons."[1]

Preaching and teaching do not have to be dull, irrelevant, irri-
tating, and uninspiring. Of course, even the best preacher and
teacher will give presentations that are better one day than another, and will give them to audiences that are more responsive
at one time than another. A good teacher or preacher, however,
must be aware of some basic principles so that he or she will give
more good presentations than poor ones. When facing the challenging task of sharing the Good News, ministers should be
aware that the task is helped or hindered by the following factors: (1) motivation; (2) personal needs; (3) preparation; (4) tim-
ing; (5) keeping reconciliation as a goal; (6) proclaiming "good
news"; (7) reality-based presentations; (8) touching souls;
(9) awareness of complexity.

MOTIVATION

Ministers should be at least reasonably motivated to give their
presentations. Ministers who teach or preach solely because it is
"their turn" are not likely to do a good job. Their motivation is
based on duty, and the accompanying effect falls somewhere between apathy and antipathy on the emotion scale of the listeners.
The dutiful minister's attitude and the listeners' attitude will be
identical: "Here we go again."

In addition to teaching and preaching out of duty, other factors
can cause motivational problems. Sometimes ministers are asked
to speak on specific topics in which they have little or no interest,
or to speak to audiences with whom they believe they have little
in common. Whatever the motivational problems, ministers
should ask themselves a serious moral question: Do I have the
right to waste the time of the five or five hundred people who will
be punished by listening to me for the next five or fifty minutes?

It is necessary that ministers be at least reasonably interested
and involved with their topic, if not brimming over with it. The
enthusiasm, sincerity, and obvious personal concern of the minister will add a significant thrust to his or her presentation, al-

though more than this is needed for generally effective communication.

PERSONAL NEEDS

Ministers who remove their personal needs (except the need to share the word of God) from their presentation will be more effective than those who do not. Even though the concept of "showing off" is usually connected with children, adults can show off just as much, although they are ordinarily less obvious about it. There is no finer opportunity to show off than when a speaker has an audience doing nothing (hopefully) except watching and listening to him or her. An audience has a high potential of awakening the "little boy" or the "little girl" in a speaker who still needs to be thought of by others as cute, comical, intelligent, strong, radical, superior, pious, sophisticated, good, or darling.

When ministers let their childish selves take over, they are simply using God as an entrée into the limelight, and their presentations are actually spiritual subterfuges. Under topic sentences such as "I'd like to share some of my reflections on the parable of the vineyard," often the subtitles would read:

- "See how I just don't talk religion but lead a deeply spiritual life."
- "See, I'm not your typical dour minister; I have a good sense of humor."
- "See, I'm not your typical wimpy do-gooder; I'm a down-to-earth regular guy."
- "See, I'm not your typical passive and demure female; I can be as strong and brilliant as any man."
- "See, I'm not your typical minister who knows only theology; I also know psychology, physics, architecture, history, and music."
- "See how great you could be if you could become like me."
- "See how cute and entertaining I am. Wouldn't you like to invite me for dinner?"

Of course, there is nothing wrong with being spiritual, being well-read, or possessing a sense of humor. When these qualities are present in a minister, they will be reflected naturally in the course of the minister's presentation. It is only when ministers, consciously or subconsciously, make a point of inserting their virtues into their presentations that problems arise. A question ministers can ask themselves is, "Is this a presentation for the Lord, or a performance for his lordship?"

PREPARATION

Ministers who prudently prepare their presentations will likely do better than those who do not. Prudent preparation means that ministers don't underprepare, that is, "wing it," or depend on an emergency transfusion of the Holy Spirit during the presentation. Students and congregations today are generally too perceptive not to notice a slipshod class or sermon when they hear one. They are also sensitive enough to be insulted by one. On the other hand, prudent preparation also means that ministers do not overprepare their presentations, because this often results in the minister becoming exhausted and bored with the topic by the time he or she presents it. Prudent preparation means that ministers do a sufficient amount of research and self-reflection so that the presentation will be sound, logical, clear, and sequential.

TIMING

Ministers must be aware of the time element in their presentations. The amount of time that an audience must sit without moving, talking, or otherwise making noise is an important consideration. As one stiff and numbed parishioner lamented, "It was a ten-minute chair and a twenty-minute sermon." Of course, because the minister is full of adrenalin, he or she is not aware of how the people who are listening to him or her feel.

Thus, the time of the presentation should be measured by how long the presentation *actually* takes and not by how long the presentation is *expected* to take. Often, presentations go significantly over the projected limit; for example, a sermon that the minister expects to take twelve minutes takes seventeen minutes, or the talk that is expected to take fifty minutes takes sixty-five minutes. For this reason, it is helpful for ministers to have, for example, five points in their outline, but also to have the talk prepared so that it can be concluded smoothly after three or four points when the projected time is elapsing.

The presentation should also be calibrated to the situation. The situation includes the age of the listeners, the level of comfort (too hot, too cold, hard chairs), the motivation of the people to hear the presentation (a captive audience or one that has come because the people are interested in the topic), and the type of service (e.g., nuptials and funerals are rarely the place for sermons that go longer than ten minutes).

KEEPING RECONCILIATION AS A GOAL

Ministers whose aim is to bring about reconciliation and redemption are more likely to be effective than those who have an ax to grind. Certainly, there are issues in which, for example, a clear injustice is being perpetrated in the community, and a minister must take a particular stand. However, such clear-cut issues are rare compared to those that *look* clear-cut because of the minister's particular vantage point.

A nonreligious example of this can be seen when watching a football game on television. Three experienced announcers, sixty thousand spectators, and millions of television viewers may see a player clearly catch a pass, until a reverse angle shot indicates that the player scooped the ball off the ground a split second before he caught it. Most important issues have two sides (labor/management, pronuclear/antinuclear, prodraft/antidraft), and when ministers take up the cause of one side against the other, they risk alienating half the listeners for no sound reason.

This does not mean important social, political, and moral issues cannot be discussed. It simply means that they can be discussed more effectively from a Christian standpoint when basic principles of love, justice, and freedom are discussed, so that people on all sides of an issue take home something to consider seriously.

Proclaiming "Good News"

Ministers who proclaim the "good news" will reach more people than those whose presentation consists of material that is neither good nor news. Presentations that threaten people (in contrast to evoking their awareness and concern) will not be perceived as good news. For example, a minister invited to speak at a graduation ceremony for an affluent private high school chose this occasion to speak on the subject "Stewardship and the Professional Person." The topic in itself could have been a good one if it had been delivered at a workshop or convention for professional people, or if the minister had treated the theme in a positive manner. In fact, what he did, however, was to lambast the graduating seniors' parents (most of whom were professional people) for charging exorbitant fees, failing to donate time and services to the poor, worshiping false gods, and foolish arrogance. Few in the audience, including the school administrators, received the message as "good news."

Along the same lines, when the same Bible stories, lives of the saints, and religious principles are rehashed week after week, month after month, year after year, it hardly qualifies as "news." Ministers who keep up with the religious literature and their personal meditations will find no dearth of ideas, topics, and themes that are "new" in the sense that people have not previously been invited to consider them. In other words, the response of listeners changes from "What else is new?" to "I've never thought of it that way."

Reality-based Presentations

Ministers who speak from their own reality-based experiences are more likely to touch people than those who speak from "theological tapes." Ministers who possess sufficient insight, honesty, and humility realize how hard it is for someone

- to turn the other cheek;
- to understand a God who allows great suffering to exist;
- to truly forgive someone who has deeply hurt him or her;
- to see God through storms of stress;

- to love people who are obnoxious;
- to genuinely sacrifice for others;
- to truly love the poor and all that it entails;
- to be honest when it means losing position or friends;
- to be humble when pride is all one has;
- to truly believe that the last will be first;
- to decline the chance for revenge;
- to treat people justly when the personal loss will be great;
- to ignore the seductions of power, prestige, or material goods;
- to control eating, drinking, drug taking, working;
- to accept traumas as "God's will";
- to struggle with one's sexuality.

Ministers who speak to people from their own human experience will be realistic, genuinely compassionate, and credible. Ministers who repress or deny their humanity, or who whitewash it, are likely to teach and preach from theological tapes. They click on a switch and go on "automatic pilot." They spew forth a staccato of spiritualisms without the slightest understanding of what they are really saying, to whom they are really saying it, and what the audience is really thinking about them. They carry on with the confidence that comes from living a risk-free life, with an unreflectiveness that comes from learning by religious rote, and with an emotionlessness that comes from a laminated heart. These ministers remind people

- of God's unconditional love, without explaining how this concept fits in with eternal damnation;
- of God's willingness to forgive, without explaining how God can be hurt in the first place;
- of the power of Satan, without explaining exactly whence this power comes, how long it will last, and why God allows it to exist;
- of God's will, without explaining how we know what God's will is and what it is not;
- of the gift of suffering, without explaining exactly why this

"gift" is necessary and what the ramifications are for people who are deprived of it;

- of the sins of secularism, without explaining how the dichotomy of the Church and the world avoids the fallacy of Platonic dualism;
- of the indissolubility of marriage, without explaining what people are supposed to do when their marriages have become psychologically and spiritually destructive;
- of the evils of lust, without explaining the important differences between lust and healthy sexual thoughts, feelings, and acts;
- of the beauty of the Church, without explaining what exactly is beautiful about the Church and what exactly is ugly about it;
- of the Church's love for its people, without explaining why the Church seems, at times, to go out of its way to make life unnecessarily difficult and painful for people;
- of the love of Jesus for the poor, without explaining if this means he loved the poor more than the wealthy and, if it does not, why the Church does not talk equally of God's love for the rich;
- of the need for redemption, without explaining why we have not already been saved totally by Christ's sacrifice;
- of the importance of Church law in our life, without explaining how this fits in with Jesus' de-emphasis of religious law;
- of the evil of the sins of pride and selfishness, without explaining the important difference between pride and healthy self-respect and between selfishness and healthy self-fulfillment;
- of the beauty of death, when Jesus did not seem to see much beauty in it.

It is important that ministers understand that the same religious concept can be either a profound and evocative thought or a meaningless spiritual slogan, depending upon what the minister brings to it. For example, the "unconditional love of God" is perhaps the greatest Christian concept. But if it is thrown to people as someone throws a bone to a dog simply to quiet its bark-

ing, the concept lacks substance and credibility. If God's unconditional love is explained in a way that people can understand,
so that they can feel its meaning in their personal lives, and if it
includes the resolution of seemingly contradictory issues, then it
becomes more than a concept; it becomes a saving event.

TOUCHING SOULS

Ministers who touch people's souls will be better instruments of
the Lord than those who irritate or soothe only the peripheral
nerve endings of people. Ministers who are well aware of and accept their fears, angers, hurts, guilts, frustrations, conflicts, pressures, hopes, failures, loneliness, joy, confusions, doubts, hypoc-
risies, manipulations, sexuality, sins, foolishness, inadequacies,
and despair are more likely to cause people to resonate with
them than than those who are out of touch with their humanity.
Ministers whose humanity is clearly present in their teaching and
preaching will strike similar chords in their listeners.

When ministers intertwine their theology with their humanity,
they can reach everyone. They do not have to worry about reaching the young people in the audience, but ignoring the old; of
getting the attention of the educated, while losing that of the uneducated; of having a message for married people, but none for
those who are single. All human beings share humanity, and it is
on this level that most good teaching and preaching occur. Henri
Nouwen describes this experience when he writes:

. . . those who listen will come to the recognition of who they really are
since the words of the preacher will find a sounding board in their own
hearts and find anchor places in their personal life experiences. And
when they allow his words to come so close as to become their flesh and
blood, they can say: "What you say loudly, I whispered in the dark;
what you pronounce so clearly, I had some suspicion about; what you
put in the foreground, I felt in the back of my mind; what you hold so
firmly in your hand always slipped away through my fingers. Yes, I find
myself in your words because your words come from the depths of human experiences and, therefore, are not just yours but also mine, and
your insights do not just belong to you, but are mine as well.[2]

AWARENESS OF COMPLEXITY

Ministers should be aware of the complexities involved both in their audiences and in the subject matter they teach.

Regarding their audiences, it is important for ministers to recognize and fully appreciate individual differences. A long tradition exists, both in the Church and in Western society, which operates on the presupposition that what is good for one person is good for everyone. In attempting to educate, counsel, and direct people, ministers often tell them what is good or bad for them, what will work or not work for them, and what will make them feel better or worse.

Paradoxically, we do not take this approach with inanimate objects or with animals, which are infinitely less complex than human beings. We realize that each piano and violin is different and, therefore, must be tuned and played differently. We recognize that each of our pets requires different food, attention, and discipline. Yet, when dealing with human beings, ministers offer advice, methodologies, and directives that are predicated on the assumption that all bodies, psyches, and souls are tuned and operate in identical ways. Obviously, it is much easier to operate on such an assumption; that is, it is easy to tell four—or four hundred—people at one time how they should live their lives. It is more difficult, but infinitely more helpful, to offer not answers or advice, but methodologies that will help people discover for themselves what may be psychologically and/or spiritually helpful for them.

It is also important for ministers to treat people appropriately, according to their ages, education, and experiences. Too frequently, ministers talk down to people. This is probably due less to an attitude of superiority than it is to the fact that the ministers were taught religion in this same way. Tape recordings of these ministers' classes, talks, workshops, or homilies would lead a listener to assume that the audience was comprised of elementary school children, when, in fact, the audience could range from bright, sophisticated high school students to adults with graduate degrees and a good deal of life experience.

For adults to be addressed as if they were children is distracting, galling, and a waste of time. Ministers should match their presentations to the audience and not the audience to their presentation. While it is admittedly difficult to target each listener's specific level of intelligence and emotional maturity, ministers should strive to hit at least the outer rings of the target.

Just as it is crucial for ministers to know *who* they teach, so it is important for ministers to understand and appreciate as fully as possible the complexities involved in *what* they teach. Ministers need to be cognizant of the ramifications, implications, and logical extensions of their teachings. This awareness stands in contrast to reeling off "taped messages" that were recorded in earlier times, passed down to the ministers, and accepted with little or no scrutiny or depth of understanding.

The following concepts are commonly and casually taught, but in reality they need a good deal of clarification and qualification in order to have any real value for people and to prevent harming them:

- "God unconditionally loves us."
- "We cannot be saved until we first ask God for forgiveness."
- "We are already saved."
- "God has a special plan for each of us."
- "We hurt God when we . . . "
- "We make God happy when we. . . "
- "God wants us to . . . "
- "We must follow what the Church teaches."
- "The bishop wants us to . . . "
- "Vows are to be kept for life."
- "It is a serious sin to . . . "

Each of these teachings is pregnant with great complexity, ambiguity, relativity, uncertainty, or error. Yet each is ordinarily taught with the same confidence and matter-of-factness with which one explains a simple problem in multiplication.

While it is true that a minister cannot offer a theological dissertation every time he or she speaks, it is also true that significant theological and psychological harm can occur from replaying "taped messages" without knowing what they mean, and what they mean to a particular audience.

PROBLEMS IN MINISTRY: AVOIDABLE AND UNAVOIDABLE

Being a Christian minister in today's world brings with it many real challenges, as well as some unnecessary tensions. The following are some examples of tensions and problems that are generally avoidable and unnecessary.

ROLE CONFUSION

Fifteen years ago the terms *role confusion* and *ministry* never would have appeared in the same book. Now there are entire books written on role confusion in ministry, almost as if the two concepts were synonymous.

William Bausch addresses role confusion with respect to Roman Catholic priests, but what he says also applies, perhaps to a lesser degree, to ministers in many Christian denominations:

There was a time when everyone knew what we meant when we said the word *priesthood*. Today, it can also mean the priesthood of all believers. Once, only the priest possessed the official ministry of the Church. Today, everyone possesses it through baptism. Once, ordination was the privileged power which conferred the fullness of the active ministry. Today, baptism takes priority and ordination is seen as an aspect of that. Once, the essense of the Catholic priesthood was seen in the personal power a male received at ordination to consecrate the eucharist and forgive sins even apart from community. Today, this is seen as departure from the first thousand years of the Church's understanding which held that presiding at the eucharist is the result, not the cause, of presiding over the community. Once, office was an automatic status conferred from above by ordination and the office bearer, by that very fact, was leader, with authority and power. Today, the functional ability and charisma of any baptized person take emotional precedence over the status of the professional clergyman as ministerial competence replaces mere status. Once, power and authority were pyramidal, moving downwards from the pope to bishops to religious to laity. Today, power and authority are respected only when seen as yielding to personal giftedness and collegiality. In short, if yesterday's world was a world wherein priesthood was well defined and pivotal and ministry of the people was vague and residual, today's world is just the opposite.[3]

Although Bausch states that not all of these concepts are necessarily true, neither are they necessarily false. Regardless of how reality-based the description is, it reflects the feeling of many ministers.

As ministers in some denominations felt their roles slip away, many became hyphenated ministers in order to regain some security and status. There were priest-psychologists, priest-lawyers, priest-physicians, priest-marriage counselors, priest-community organizers, etc. However, it seems that many of these ministers became unhyphenated by leaving the ministry altogether or by leaving their second field of endeavor and returning to full-time ministry.

Whatever attempts ministers have made to reduce role confusion, a certain degree of it still remains ("What exactly is my role?" "How is it different than any other Christian's?"). In attempting to address this problem, it may be helpful to consider a somewhat analogous situation.

Fifty years ago, physicians claimed the sole right and responsibility to diagnose and treat anyone who was physically or psychologically ill. Since then, the medical pie has been cut up into several pieces. Now there are licensed psychologists, nurse practitioners, midwives, public health professionals, nutritionists, psychiatric social workers, physiotherapists, alcohol and drug counselors, marriage and family counselors, chiropractors, osteopaths, podiatrists, and optometrists.

Every time one of these professions fought for and was granted independent status and privileges, the medical profession (as a group) was threatened in terms of power, prestige, and income. Yet, it is doubtful that a single physician left medicine or became a hyphenated physician as a result of being forced to share power and roles with nonphysicians. One basic reason for this is that physicians realized that their aim was to help the suffering, and there was plenty of work to go around. Even with the allied professions mentioned above, there are millions of people in the United States alone without proper medical and psychological care. Furthermore, the sharing of the medical pie created little, if any, role confusion. For example, although the roles of psychologists and psychiatrists overlap about ninety percent, and although they squabble over turf rights, neither group experiences doubt or confusion about who they are, what their work is, what their worth is, or what their values are.

Returning to the role confusion in ministry, one is forced to wonder why, if ministers are primarily interested in helping people spiritually and not in their own power, prestige, or privileges, there is role confusion. There is certainly a sufficient number of souls to go around. This would be true even if the day should come when nonordained ministers were permitted to administer all of the sacraments and the roles of ordained and nonordained ministers were to overlap by ninety percent.

One is left with the distinct impression that ministers who are confused, discouraged, or resentful because the ministerial pie is being shared are those who recognize neither the beauty of their calling nor the limitless need for their services. If the goal of ministers is to heal souls, there can never be enough ministers; if the goal is to be elite, then there are always too many of them.

LONELINESS

There are basically three kinds of loneliness: existential, situational, and self-imposed. Existential loneliness stems from our uniqueness and separateness and creates a void in us that cannot be filled on earth. Though we can be in intimate relationships, be close to our parents, be married, have children, and have many close friends, none of these can make two spirits become one. The degree to which two spirits do not completely overlap reflects the size of the existential vacuum. Two people can become as close as people can be, yet neither becomes the other or fills the other. As the saying goes: "We are born alone and die alone" (and face God alone—not with our beloved spouse, children, parents, or friends). Since *all* people experience existential loneliness, this would not account for a minister feeling more lonely than other people.

When we stand naked and alone, apart from the people we love the most and the things we like best to do, we are exposed to an important dimension of our existence. And it is this void and the questions and emotions that flow from it that give substance and direction to life. Attempting to fill the void distracts us from our uniqueness, purpose, frailty, and dependence on the hope of a life hereafter.

Situational loneliness occurs when a minister truly wants to relate with people in mutually fulfilling ways, but there is little or no opportunity to do so, at least during a particular period of time. For example, a minister who is sent to a new parish, away from friends and relatives, may well experience loneliness until he or she can cultivate new relationships. However, these periods of loneliness are usually short-lived and rarely cause problems.

A third kind of loneliness is self-imposed; that is, the minister causes his or her own loneliness. This can occur in three ways. First, ministers who are, consciously or unconsciously, insecure or frightened may protect themselves with a psychological moat over which few, if any, people are allowed to pass. These ministers are fearful that if they allow another person to get close to them, they will be rejected or will lose control to the other person. Insecure or frightened ministers also may relate to people in ways that are condescending, critical, or manipulating, which pushes people away and leads to loneliness.

Second, ministers who are, consciously or unconsciously, angry (frustrated, resentful, disappointed) can create a no-man's-land between themselves and others as a shield against their anger being ignited. Although this "demilitarized zone" affords security, it also creates loneliness. Angry ministers may also relate to people in ways that are sarcastic, intimidating, or demeaning, which causes people to keep their distance, and also causes loneliness.

Third, for whatever reasons, some ministers harbor the misconception that they cannot allow themselves to get close to anyone because it will somehow make them less effective as ministers. What they are really saying is that they cannot allow themselves to be loved or to love because this love will interfere with their ministry of love. In fact, however, it is not only possible for ministers to be in love relationships and be effective ministers, it is a requirement. If the person with whom the minister is close needs objective, third-party help, it is easy to make a proper referral. Ministry can never be used as an excuse not to be in love with people, and when it is, the problem does not lie with the ministry but with the minister.

Loneliness can be directly experienced by a minister, or it can come in a variety of disguises. Both cases cry out for remedy, and in either case, the conscious and unconscious remedies often consist of getting into intense nonhuman relationships as substitutes for intimate human relationships. Some examples of intense nonhuman relationships include becoming overinvolved in work, pleasure, sex, avocations, material possessions, pets, alcohol, drugs, eating, and even prayer. These relationships can become as strong as—even stronger than—any human relationship and, at least temporarily, kill the pain of loneliness.

However, problems accompany these nonhuman relationships. First of all, the stronger the nonhuman relationship, the further the minister moves away from human relationships. Also, most of the nonhuman relationships that are pursued with intensity cause problems of their own, for example, relationships with work, food, drink, sex, etc. And finally, nonhuman relationships are not adequate substitutes for interpersonal intimacy and, therefore, do not have the salutory effects of such intimacy.

Although all ministers, by virtue of their being human, are lonely, the greater portion of the lonely minister's problem is self-imposed and not an inherent part of being a minister. The fact that there are many ministers, including celibate ministers, who are not inordinately lonely (and that there are married ministers who *are* inordinately lonely), points to the fact that ministry and loneliness are not inherently related. Ministers whose loneliness is interfering with their sense of well-being should seek the psychological and/or spiritual help they need to free themselves of their self-imposed condition.

A PLURALITY OF PHILOSOPHIES AND THEOLOGIES

Twenty-five years ago there were relatively few operative philosophies and theologies in ministry ("operative" means those that were directly or indirectly referred to on a daily basis by ministers). The typical minister had been educated according to thinkers such as Aristotle, Aquinas, Scotus, Luther, Calvin, and Wesley, and believed that their philosophical and theological knowledge pretty well covered the spectrum of all relevant issues, human and divine.

Today, however, there is a plurality of philosophies and theologies along with a plurality of methodologies within each discipline. Issues that were crystal clear a quarter century ago now have become far less clear. The certitude of the past has become the confusion of the present.

These changes have taken place because of a more enlightened understanding of Scripture, Church history, tradition, revelation, theology, philosophy, and human behavior. As a result, some "absolute truths" have become less absolute; some "eternal values" have become more time-limited; the "truth" has become "the truths"; and "Church authority" has become "Church authorities."

The effects of these philosophical and theological modifications have been varied. Some ministers grew nicely and comfortably along with the changes; others entrenched themselves in the philosophy and theology of their seminary days; still others gave up in despair, creating *ad hoc* philosophies and theologies that seemed to change on a seasonal, if not a daily basis.

The true cause of the confusion, anxiety, and, in some instances, antipathy, was not the new pluralism itself but the old supposition that, by the sixteenth century, "Truth" was captured once and for all. As a result, for the past five hundred years Christians have used the same philosophical and theological sextant to maintain a proper course. As the sextant became calibrated differently in the last quarter century, many Christians, ministers included, became disoriented and lost.

However, if one accepts the supposition that truth is not static but evolutionary, then pluralism is not only expected, it is also put to good use. Perhaps we find no better example of this than in the field of psychology, where, at last count, there are more than two hundred and fifty theories of counseling.[4] Yet, this pluralism not only does *not* create confusion and anxiety, but is welcomed as providing new and different tools for pursuing truth.

There is no legitimate reason why the same can not be true for Christianity. Once we overcome the prejudice that there is only one clearly defined set of eternal Christian truths, the rest is relatively easy. Without sliding into privatism, ministers can weave sound theological and philosophical principles together with sound psychological, sociological, and anthropological principles, along with their own being, experience, and situation, and form an ever-expanding fabric of Christian endeavor. As Charles Curran states:

Ultimately the individual minister himself must responsibly fashion his own ministerial role in terms of the people he is trying to serve and the circumstances in which he finds himself. The Word and Work of Jesus can take on innumerable forms. Theology can and should provide broad guidelines and offer criticisms, but ultimately the concrete meaning of ministry comes from the minister himself.[5]

Of course, this requires infinitely more time, energy, study, insight, freedom, security, and openness than does having one philosophical tome and one theological tome from which all answers flow. Nevertheless, it is also infinitely more valid, vibrant, and rewarding.

PROFESSIONAL INSECURITY

In their most honest and reflective moments, many ministers question the importance and efficacy of their work. Furthermore, both the nonreligious and the religious environments in which they work often reinforce their doubts. As hospital chaplains, ministers may be barely tolerated by busy physicians and nurses, and many ministers feel that their services pale in the light of the dramatic, lifesaving performances of the medical professions. In the military, ministers may be derisively referred to as "sky pilots" who deal mostly with "crybabies." As prison chaplains, ministers often feel more like messengers for the inmates than ministers of the Lord.

Even in religious environments, ministers may be viewed as shamans, who are spiritually well connected, or as theological teddy bears, who are cute and comfortable to have around. Moreover, even within the ministry itself, ministers can be treated as children by their superiors and as stupid, peculiar, or out-of-touch by their peers.

When facing periods of self-questioning and lack of respect from others, ministers may consider the following points: ministry's rewards are nonmaterial; the work of ministry is complex; and in ministry it is all right not to feel "professionally" all right.

Because ministry deals with the nonmaterial, it will never earn the respect of those who prize the material. The vast majority of ministers will not be wealthy, will not perform dramatic feats, such as saving a life, saving an innocent person from going to jail, or designing a symphony hall, and will not possess professional, social, or political clout. Because male ministers cannot allow themselves to become "one of the boys," their masculinity may be somewhat suspect, and because female ministers are not seen as "one of the girls," they may be viewed as uppity. In the eyes of those who rate material values highly, ministry will always be a second-rate profession, which is a positive sign. A problem arises only when ministers judge their worth and effectiveness by the same criteria used by those who prioritize material success.

Dealing with the spiritual life and welfare of people is ordinarily far more complex and challenging than dealing with either the body or the psyche. When people have a medical or psychological problem, they often are aware of the accompanying pain or distress, and sooner or later take steps to seek some sort of healing. However, it seems hardly arguable that the vast majority of people have spiritual problems, at least in the form of spiritual anemia, but do not have the slightest awareness of their illness. And when a crisis occurs that forces them to come in contact with a minister, they may become hostile toward the minister (whom they perceive as an ambassador of a terrible God), or they may seek the minister for his or her magical powers. In either case, ministers have their work cut out for them.

A certain degree of professional insecurity in ministry may, at times, be appropriate. Some, or perhaps many, ministers are undereducated, which does not mean uneducated. Undereducated means that ministers attempt to be effective in situations for which they have been inadequately educated and trained. They fail to keep current with the literature, and their formal, continuing education consists of attending a one-day workshop or reading a couple of books each year, if it consists of anything. Compare this with the at least weekly perusal of relevant literature by physicians, attorneys, professors, and other professionals, and to the continuing education required by the state and professional organizations of many professions. Therefore, as a result of being undereducated, the minister's teaching can be anachronistic, his or her preaching may be uninspiring, and his or her counseling is likely to be simplistic. This, in turn, diminishes both the respect of others and the minister's sense of personal effectiveness.

In summary, there is no valid reason for ministers to feel like second-class helpers. Ministers should not want to earn the respect of materially minded people. They should realize that their work requires at least the skills, patience, and fortitude of a physician, psychologist, or attorney. If their professional insecurity is appropriate because they are not up-to-date with their profession, they can solve this problem by taking the appropriate steps to upgrade their abilities.

PERCEPTIONS THAT CAN CAUSE OR PREVENT BURNOUT IN MINISTRY

When an automobile is driven more than the amount of lubrication in the engine allows, the engine will burn out, and the automobile will come to a stop. Analogously, when ministers suffer burnout, it means that the amount of stress (frustration, pressure, conflict) they experience is significantly more than their stress-modifying behavior.

BASIC CONSIDERATIONS

It is important to note that the cause of burnout is not overwork. Burnout is caused by the unequal balance between stress and behavior that prevents and reduces stress. In other words, some ministers could work significantly less than others and still suffer burnout because they lack an adequate amount of stress-modifying behaviors to absorb their level of work stress. This accounts for a situation in which two ministers are under equal amounts of stress but one minister thrives and grows as a result of the stress while the other burns out.

It is also important to distinguish between job stress and vocational stress. A minister may be in the right vocation but simply not be handling the work aspects of it well. Another minister's stress may stem from the psychosocial stress inherent in being a minister, even though he or she is handling the job stress reasonably well. When this distinction is not made, some ministers who experience burnout will leave the ministry when all they needed was to change some simple work-related behavior patterns. Other ministers remain in the ministry and, although they change some behavior patterns with respect to their work, continue to experience burnout.

Generally, it is better to assume that the symptoms of burnout stem from one's approach to work and directly related issues. If changes in this area reduce or extinguish the symptoms, then it is clear that the area of work was the cause of the short-circuit. If, on the other hand, informal and formal help do little to reduce the symptoms over a reasonable period of time, then the assumption can be made that the area of vocation, and not work, is the problem.

Another note of importance is that, while the term "burnout" is relatively new, the phenomenon of burnout is as old as the human race. Burnout is not simply a fad or an excuse to take a sabbatical. Just as an automobile engine burning out can be very serious, psyche and spirit burnout can be comparably as serious. Ministers who suffer third-degree burnout may never be able to function properly again, in or out of the ministry.

Thus, it is important to note that when symptoms of burnout do occur, it is very unusual for the minister to recognize the symptoms as a warning. The minister may temporarily slow down or take a little time off, but it is rare that the minister will make a permanent change in his or her personality and/or work patterns. Sadly, when basic changes are not made, the same symptoms will recur.

A final note of importance is that the body, psyche, and soul are intertwined in such a way that what negatively affects one necessarily negatively affects the other two. It should be clear by this point that the old belief that God will provide as long as a person is doing God's work is fallacious, unless taking care of one's own body and psyche is included as part of God's work.

SIGNS OF BURNOUT

The following are some common signs or indicators of ministry burnout. It is important that ministers recognize these signs for what they are—warning signals that their ministry is in trouble:

- decreasing interest in one's daily work or in one's overall ministry;
- decreasing energy to perform tasks that were once relatively easy to perform;
- decreasing enjoyment in experiences that were once enjoyable, for example, preparing sermons, playing golf, etc.;
- decreasing carefulness in personal habits, such as in dress, grooming, hygiene, punctuality, conscientiousness;
- decreasing feelings of renewal after experiences which were once revitalizing, for example, enjoying a day off with a friend, visiting one's family, etc.;
- increasing cynicism and pessimism with respect to one's effec-

tiveness, to the general worth of one's ministry or life-style or to people in general;

- increasing behavioral symptoms of anxiety: difficulty concentrating, forgetfulness, "tuning out" people, inability to sit still, need to distract oneself, trouble listening to people, cutting appointments short;
- increasing psychophysiological symptoms of anxiety: tension headaches, muscle tightness, high blood pressure, insomnia, frequent colds, undiagnosable complaints, chronic fatigue, dizziness, indigestion, tightness in chest, hyperventilation, hand tremors, perspiring;
- an increase in interpersonal difficulties: being sarcastic, irritable, impatient, hostile, resentful, rude, withdrawn;
- an increase in anesthetic behaviors: eating, drinking, drugging, sleeping, or using sex in inappropriate or destructive ways, in order to dull the pain of stress.

Each of the above signs of burnout may be experienced mildly, moderately, or severely; and the extent of ministerial impairment they signal may likewise be mild, moderate, or severe. Regardless of the level of impairment, each sign is a symptom of a ministerial malady whose cause must be diagnosed before the disease can be cured.

CAUSES OF BURNOUT

There are several ways to describe the causes of burnout. However, we will deal with two generic causes: the perception of oneself and the perception of others.

With regard to self-perception, ministers who do not burn out differ from those who do in at least three ways.

In the first place, ministers who do not burn out define their worth not by how much they do, but by who they are. For the most part, they realize that they are kind, compassionate, sensitive, unselfish, honest, and moral. They understand that a minister could accomplish a prodigious number of tasks each day, yet be significantly lacking in these qualities. In fact, they have discovered that when they do overextend themselves, those qualities diminish in direct proportion to their overwork. They also recognize that it is not how much work they do, but how they do it, which enables them to set limits and to say no to people without feeling less worthwhile or virtuous.

Ministers who burn out tend to define their worth by their work: the more they accomplish, the more worthwhile they are. This causes problems on several fronts. First, such ministers place themselves in an impossible double bind: if they do not work continually, they feel less worthwhile and increasingly guilty; if they do overwork, they eventually become fragmented and exhausted. Second, such ministers are like cups with a hole in the bottom. When they overwork during the day, they go to bed with a full cup of self-worth and feel satisfied with themselves. However, the self-worth seeps out of the cup during the night, and they awake with an empty cup. And the cycle begins all over again. Third, these ministers do not easily take full days off or vacations, because during the time they are not working, they are losing important self-worth points. Consequently, they often work on holidays and even when they are ill. The only time they feel justified not working is when a physician orders them to bed or to take time off. Fourth, because they are typically harried, such ministers do not have time to enjoy relationships which would touch them in ways that reflect their true worth. They are like physicians who are so busy treating large numbers of patients that they rarely have time to enjoy their families or the human, personal parts of their relationships with their patients, experiences that would reflect their genuine worth.[6]

The second way in which ministers who do not suffer burnout differ from those who do is by keeping a realistic perception of their abilities and limitations. They recognize that they can be helpful to some people but not to all people, and that they can give of themselves sometimes but not all of the time. As a result, they refer people to other ministers or professionals who can be of more help because of their training, experience, or amount of available time. Healthy ministers do this not in an apologetic, guilty fashion, but in the same manner that all professionals make intelligent and appropriate referrals. Their realistic perception also enables them to have a keen sense of when their cup is beginning to brim over with stress, and they are able to say, "That's all for now, thanks," just as they do when a waitress is filling their coffee cup.

Ministers who burn out, on the other hand, perceive themselves as trying to be "all things to all people." This attitude is a throwback to the days when ministers were trained to have a messiah complex, to serve as factotums who helped people find jobs, treated alcoholics, gave advice on childrearing, kept people out of jail, got elderly people into homes for the aged, and held marriages together. It is also a throwback to a theology that, at least on an operational level, held that God entrusted the souls in the parish to the minister and that, in some sense, the minister was responsible or accountable for them. Consequently, ministers felt they had to be on call twenty-four hours each day and had to be present at all crises and celebrations.

However, the reality is that the "all things to all people" tape has not been played in the Church for some time. So why do some ministers thread it into their tape player every day, while other ministers have destroyed it long ago? The answer is that some ministers need to play the tape because it makes them feel important and needed, and it distracts them from facing more difficult issues, such as the fear of intimacy, sexual confusion, an anemic spiritual life, interpersonal conflicts, and loneliness.

The third difference in the perception of self between ministers who do not burn out and those who do is that ministers who do not burn out perceive themselves in an accepting and positive light, and they treat themselves as they would treat a dear friend. They take adequate leisure time (at last two or three hours each day) and use it well (doing enjoyable things). They admit and communicate their feelings to the appropriate person at the time they experience the feelings, or at least before the day is finished, so that they go to bed with a clean emotional slate. They get their needs for security, support, love, esteem, solitude, freedom, and joy met in their personal lives, and they extricate themselves as constructively as possible from intractably destructive situations and relationships.

Ministers who burn out, however, tend to treat themselves poorly. They overwork, and when they do take time off work, they are as likely to use it poorly (running errands for the better part of the day) as to use it well. They hold in feelings of hurt, fear, anger, guilt, sexuality, confusion, and loneliness, which causes these feelings to fester and toxify their bodies and souls. They ignore and demean their personal needs and, therefore, live a life of semistarvation. They remain entrapped in draining and damaging relationships, which further sap their few psychological resources.

The second generic cause of ministerial burnout is rooted in the differing ways ministers tend to perceive others. Ministers who do not burn out realize that the vast majority of people have the ability to handle problems, crises, and traumas by themselves and/or with the support of relatives and friends. Furthermore, these ministers realize that the vast majority of people who experience a crisis actually prefer to be left alone with themselves and those closest to them. Although most people appreciate the well-intentioned attempts by outsiders (including ministers) to help them, they often experience such attempts as more intrusive than helpful. Realizing this, ministers who do not tend to burn out will communicate their concern and offer their services to people experiencing a crisis, either by dropping a note or by a telephone call. This genuine invitation is one which people can feel equally free to accept or decline. This approach not only expresses the minister's concern, but it also frees people to decide whether or not to invite the minister into their lives during their crisis period.

Ministers who burn out, however, tend to adhere to the delusion that all people in crisis need a minister (or some outside help). These ministers dash into people's lives uninvited, often saying and doing things that are meaningless to the people or that actually increase people's already heightened levels of tension and stress. Of course, people will be polite to these ministers

and thank them for all their "help." Unfortunately, such responses only reinforce the ministers' delusion.

In fact, ministers who are burdened with this delusion will find
themselves crisis-hopping, that is, scurrying from one crisis to
another, one home to another, one hospital bed to another. They
may even enjoy it, but because these encounters are very draining and because such excursions are fatiguing and often stressful
in themselves, it is typical that these ministers eventually burn
out, and, unfortunately, they do so in a dubious cause.

A second difference in the perception of others between ministers who do not burn out and those who do is that ministers who
do not burn out expect some people to be upset with them. These
ministers place the upset person's agitation in a realistic perspective and do not let it negatively influence them. They realize that
there are times when they must say, "I'm sorry, but I won't be
able to officiate at your daughter's wedding," or "I'm sorry. I
won't be able to see you for spiritual direction, but I can refer you
to someone who is as competent as I, if not more so."

These ministers also realize that there are times when they
must set limits and say no to people. These times include when
the ministers cannot afford to accept one more stress, responsibility, or pressure in their lives; when they must prioritize pastoral activities (e.g., deciding that giving a presentation on pastoral
care is more important than presiding at someone's marriage);
when they lack the motivation or competency to help a particular
person with a particular problem; when they have planned a
holiday that is *necessary* to take. Healthy ministers also realize
that some people will react to their "no" with anger and resentment that will be manifested inappropriately: public complaints
about the minister; periods of pouting and hurt feelings; and
even rejection. However, these ministers also realize that they
must set limits on their time and energy, and that they cannot allow the anticipated negative reactions of people to force them
into poor decisions.

Consciously and/or unconsciously, ministers who burn out
tend to be inordinately swayed by what others think and feel

about them. These ministers are professional nice guys who sub-sist on daily doses of acceptance and affirmation. They tend to Christianize what is, in actuality, a narcissistic need to feel liked by assuring themselves and others that their selflessness is sim-ply a manifestation of their Christian commitment. Upsetting even one person is avoided with the same intensity as a drug ad-dict avoids upsetting his or her supplier.

The worst thing that could befall these ministers is to have someone complain to others about them, especially to those in au-thority. These ministers feel that if they say no to some people, the people will not only be disappointed, but will perceive the minis-ter as selfish, lazy, insensitive, arrogant, or unappreciative, and will announce their upsetting experience to anyone who will lis-ten. Thus, these ministers are imminently open to blackmail, and they compulsively dance to any and all tunes, lest someone be-come disgruntled with them. Of course, dancing day and night to every possible melody eventually becomes exhausting, and the only way to sit out a dance with permission is to become physical-ly or psychologically sick, which these ministers eventually do.

A third, and final, difference between the ways others are per-ceived by ministers who do not burn out and those who do is that ministers who do not burn out view people simply as people and not as means to an end. Ministers who burn out tend to view people as stepping-stones to something better. They may view people as

- spiritual stepping-stones (the more people a minister helps, the higher the minister's place in heaven);
- material stepping-stones (the more parish and personal dona-tions the minister will receive);
- social stepping-stones (the more friends and social life the minister will have);
- career stepping-stones (the higher up the promotional ladder the minister will go).

Of course, no one consciously perceives people as stepping-stones, but the telltale signs of this mentality eventually become apparent. People who can directly or indirectly do something for the minister are catered to, and when they can no longer be helpful, they are discarded. The problem is that such ministers never stop using others as stepping-stones. Although one specific stone may no longer be needed, there is always another one to take its place. Consequently, these ministers are always hopping from one stone to the next, seeking something or other from people who they perceive will make them happier. Since this is an endless pursuit, exhaustion is often the eventuality.

In summary, ministers need to be aware of the danger of self-fulfilling prophecies. The ways ministers perceive themselves and others will either add to or alleviate stress. This is not to say that there are not some specific sources of stress in ministry (e.g., repetitive, draining, endless, and often unappreciated work), for indeed there are. However, ministers must keep in mind, first of all, that these stresses are not unique to ministry. Physicians, police officers, counselors, fire fighters, probation officers, community organizers, teachers—especially those in inner-city schools—parents in general, and parents of large families in particular all experience as much, if not more, objective stress as do ministers.

Secondly, ministers should realize that the kind or degree of objective stress in a person's life rarely causes burnout. It is far more common that it is a person's subjective reaction to the stress and his or her overall life-style that determine whether or not a person experiences burnout.

Finally, ministers can also be heartened by the fact that the vast majority of ministers do not suffer from burnout. Indeed, the majority of ministers have realistic perceptions of themselves and others. If burnout was an inherent part of ministry, this would not be true.

PRAYER AS A RESOURCE IN MINISTRY

It is often stated that a minister should have a good prayer life, but rarely is the distinction made between a good and a problematic prayer life. Rather, it is assumed that all ways of praying are equally efficacious with respect both to the personal and professional growth of the minister and to the minister's relationship with God. This section deals with how prayer can be a vital resource in a minister's life.

TALKING TO GOD AND PRAYING ARE NOT NECESSARILY SYNONYMOUS

If prayer is to be a dynamic resource in ministry, ministers must first recognize that prayer is more than talking to God. Just as there can be a great difference between *talking to* and *communicating with* one's friend, there can be a great difference between talking to and communicating with God. One key to the difference lies in the effects of the two types of interchange. When people talk *to* each other, it is rare for either person to undergo any change. When people communicate *with* each other, it is typical for some change to take place. The change may be significant, or it may be imperceptible to the naked eye; nevertheless, some change is forthcoming. As Gerard Fourez writes:

To test whether prayer revolves around self-delusion, examine its fruits. If someone spends time at prayer and begins to be afraid of people and of God, if he tends to draw away from relationships with people, if he becomes less aware of social needs, then he should examine the validity of his prayer life. If prayer does not make people freer or happier or more open to Christian liberation, this prayer is not bearing fruit. On the contrary, if prayer helps people to be freer, more at ease with themselves and others, if they feel more love and experience more openness, then prayer is bearing fruit. This, practically speaking, is the way to judge the authenticity of prayer—in terms of its individual human consequence.[7]

In other words, it is important to discover whether the prayer is simply an echo of the minister talking to himself or herself, or an authentic dialogue between the minister and God.

Ministers can find themselves *talking to God* for a variety of reasons: to feel more secure, to feel more righteous, to get the edge on other people, to ratify the way they are doing things. But when talking to God involves little or no critical reflection or listening, prayer becomes a meaningless exercise.

Specifically, authentic communication with God can be expected to bring about changes in the minister. Because authentic communication makes us become more aware of our imperfections and our weaknesses—the hurt we caused others, our neglect of others, our insensitivity, our ignorance—it increases our humility and decreases our arrogance.

Authentic communication makes us aware of our own mortality and helps us stop living as if we will never die. Although we all know intellectually that we are going to die relatively soon, we do not behave as if we truly believe it. In fact, although as Christians we believe that we will evolve to an infinitely better state, as human beings most of us would just as soon stay right where we are, even if our lot is an unhappy one. Authentic prayer helps us realize that we are not going to remain as we are, and the more fully we realize this, the more we can live each day the way it should be lived. We are also more apt to tell people how much we love them and how sorry we are that we have not adequately communicated and expressed this love in the past. Finally, the recognition of our mortality brought about by authentic prayer makes us more apt to go out of our way to help people, to be less quick to condemn, more likely to live each day fully, and free to act according to what we need for our growth.

Authentic prayer increases our appreciation of existential and spiritual values and decreases our concerns over material strivings. We become more aware of what *sic transit gloria mundi* means. We are less distracted by our needs for a bigger house, an extra car, the next promotion, party, romance, gourmet meal, vacation, or accolade; and we get more in touch with the spiritual gifts we already possess and with those that are within our reach.

Authentic prayer increases our awareness of injustice, and of the needless and destructive suffering of others. Once we become more aware of human destruction, we want to do something about it, and are no longer content to ignore suffering or shake our heads in despair. Even though we may know that whatever we do may be but a drop in the bucket, we make the effort because we also know that the cause is worth it.

Authentic prayer increases our courage and strength and decreases our fear and pessimism. We find that we are more open

about our beliefs, less apt to speak or act merely to gain acceptance, and that we are more open to, and concerned about, clearly and constructively reflecting (i.e., living out) our values.

Finally, authentic prayer (i.e., communication *with* God) increases our freedom, both personal and interpersonal, and decreases our needs to repress ourselves and others. We allow ourselves a wider range of thoughts, feelings, and activities, and we
allow others to think, feel, and act along lines that they feel are
best suited to them. We have less need to conform and to make
others conform simply because conformity reduces our anxiety.

Talking *to* God reinforces sameness and staleness. Communicating *with* God yields fruits that are observable to oneself and
others. It is important for Christians, and especially Christian
ministers, to recognize the difference.

PRAYER IS MORE THAN ASKING GOD FOR SOMETHING

Just as prayer is not simply a one-way communication, neither is
it simply petitionary in nature. That is, to be a vital resource in
ministry, prayer must be an activity in which we engage, not simply to make requests; a response to God's intimacy, not simply a
petition for God's favor.

Regarding prayer of petition, Karl Rahner writes:

> We call on Him as we would to our insurance office; we pay grudgingly
> as we wait eagerly for our bonus. Our hands outstretched in prayer are
> mercenary hands; they show a certain near-parody of spiritual eagerness
> only when we are asking for something. This, of course, though witness-
> ing to that hardening of the spiritual arteries we spoke of, is better than
> complete spiritual sclerosis. But what a travesty of prayer it really is! It is
> surely but the odour of an empty vase.[8]

Although perhaps understating the legitimacy of prayers of petition, Rahner's point is well-taken; namely, when prayer is limited
to asking for favors, it is to the real disadvantage of the person
praying. Analogously, a child who relates to a parent with enthusiasm only when asking for something will experience but a
minimal opportunity to grow psychologically and spiritually.

Prayer that is real communication *with* God possesses many of the qualities of real communication between people. Using the analogy of asking a friend for a favor may help us discover some important questions we can ask ourselves about prayers of petition.

First, should I ask a friend for a favor out of sheer laziness, that is, ask him to do for me what it would be more appropriate and strengthening to do for myself? In other words, should I pray that God will make my ministry more fruitful without my expending effort to better it myself?

Secondly, should I ask a friend a favor that she is unlikely to grant, thus creating hurt and tension between us? Should I ask God to get me into graduate school, even though it would be unjust to other students if I were accepted because my grades or motivation are not as high as theirs?

Third, should I ask a friend for a favor, when granting such a favor may be injurious to others? In other words, should I pray that my niece will not marry a certain man because his religion, race, education, or personality do not fit my dream for her, even though they seem to have at least a reasonably good relationship and are in love with each other?

Fourth, should I ask a friend for a favor, when, if it were granted, I would be deprived of an experience which I need for growth? Should I ask God to save me from the consequences of some injudicious behavior, even though it would be to my ultimate advantage to experience them?

Lastly, should I ask a friend for a favor under the direct or indirect threat of retribution if the favor is not granted? Should I tell God: "God, the only thing I really want is to have my own parish. Please grant my wish, especially if you want my help, love, and loyalty in the future?"

Staying with the analogy of friendship, ministers can realize that we communicate with our friends for reasons beyond asking favors. So, too, should we communicate with God. For example, I want to tell my friend how much I love and appreciate him. He may not *need* to be told this, but *I* may need to tell him this. When I share my affection with another, I grow closer to that person, and more loving toward myself and others.

When I have done something that has placed a distance between myself and my friend, I want to tell my friend that I'm sorry. I discuss how the situation occurred, where I was remiss, what I learned from it; then I forgive myself, and ask my friend's forgiveness.

I turn to my friend for honest feedback. Too many people give me feedback that is overly positive or overly negative. I want to share my innermost self and know that what comes back to me comes from a completely trusting relationship.

I want to share thoughts and feelings that I cannot share with someone else—that I am confused, jealous, resentful, inadequate, frightened, guilty, hurt, in love, sinful, lonely, or sick. But I want to share them with someone who will understand them and not simply respond, "You shouldn't feel that way," or, "It's all right to feel that way." I want to share my innermost self in ways that will make a difference in my life.

Such active and responsive communication is as important in our relationship with God as it is in our relationship with our closest friend. Ministers need to keep in touch with their close friends *and* to keep in touch with God. Realistically, however, sometimes ministers feel close to God, and at other times, very distant. Sometimes ministers can feel a deep sense of love for God, and at other times, they may feel a deep sense of isolation, if not alienation. This happens because human beings are not created in ways that allow them to bask in either human or divine intimacy for long periods of time; therefore, ministers can expect the same types and degrees of distance to occur in their relationship with God as occur in their relationships with friends. What is essential to both relationships—what keeps them both alive in good times and in bad—is active and responsive communication.

The Necessity for Silence and Prayerful Meditation

All open, active, and responsive communication takes time. It takes time to establish deep friendship and time to nourish it. We Christians believe that God extends a welcome to our friendship, that God initiates it. It is up to us to nurture that relationship with our attention and time. Therefore, ministers need to give themselves and God time on an ongoing basis. Ministers need to guarantee themselves regular periods of silence and meditation in which they have the time to discover the inner signals that can lead them closer to God and to others.

In today's world, however, it appears almost impossible to enjoy periods of silence and meditation. Seemingly endless responsibilities and stresses keep people's minds and hearts in a constant state of distraction and activity. Such frenetic and ceaseless activity creates a serious problem that is analogous to that of a potential rescuer attempting to pick up the static-filled radio signals of a ship foundering at sea. The more static in the signal, the less contact possible between ship and shore, which increases the likelihood that the ship will stray farther and become irretrievably lost. Our "shore" is our inner self; it houses our deepest needs, values, and hopes, which ordinarily are directional signals to a reasonably happy and harmonious life.

To keep contact with these signals, ministers need to ensure for themselves daily periods of silence and inner reflection. Doing so is not unlike beginning each day of a trip by spending time checking the map to see where one wishes to go and what routes will best get one there. With such reference points clearly in mind, the traveler is better able to make the correct choice at each juncture.

By affording themselves daily periods of silence, ministers can clear the static that may be jamming their signals. Then self-reflection and self-evaluation can occur. This, in turn, provides ministers a navigational check as to the course they are on and whether or not it should be altered.

In their daily periods of silence, ministers may wish to ask themselves self-reflective questions similar to the following:

• Am I being honest, fair, just, and freeing to myself, my family and loved ones, my friends, my fellow workers, and the people I serve?

- Am I living according to my values, and am I becoming the kind of person my best self always wanted to become?
- Is my relationship with God and the Church what I would like it to be?
- If I am on course, what can I do today to continue my course with even sharper precision?
- If I am straying off course in one or more areas, what can I do today to return to the proper course?

When ministers protest that they do not have the luxury of taking time (fifteen to thirty minutes) out of their day for themselves, they ignore three realities: first, meditation is not a luxury, it is a necessity; second, without such personal time, ministers often waste far more time frantically running around because they did not get their existential, religious, and material priorities straight ahead of time; third, the same ministers who do not have half an hour to spare for meditation often have lots of time to waste.

Ministers who have gone on retreats, especially those that last for a week or more, are familiar with what getting in touch with one's real, true, or basic self means. However, while retreats are certainly worthwhile, a yearly retreat made in lieu of daily or near-daily meditation is like dieting or jogging for only one or two weeks each year. It is better than nothing, but it does not take the place of daily attention to one's health. So, too, regular periods of meditation help ministers pay attention to the health of their relationship with their inner selves and with God.

In summary, it is essential that ministers work to foster and maintain a good prayer life. To be judged "good," a minister's prayer life must be based on authentic communication *with* God that leads both to self-awareness and to deeper awareness of God in his or her life. To be judged "good," a minister's prayer life must be composed of more than petitions for God's graciousness; it must be a life lived in a way that acknowledges God's gracious friendship. Finally, to be judged "good," a minister's prayer life must be worth the minister's lavishing upon it that precious commodity, time; it must be worth the silence and reflection needed to respond to one's own internal signals and to the guiding voice of God. Only then will prayer be a vital resource in a minister's life. Only then may a minister's prayer life be called "good."

4. Dealing with Sexual Issues

The purpose of this chapter is to offer some information, ideas, and principles to help ministers deal effectively with some of the sexual issues they will be asked to address in the world today. Things have changed dramatically in the area of sexuality over the last twenty years. A relatively short time ago, it was easy for ministers to deal with sexual issues: typically, ministers simply echoed what the Church said and what they believed the Bible taught. As a result, two groups evolved: The first group was made up of "good" Christians who unquestioningly obeyed the teachings of the Church, no matter what the cost. The second group was comprised of "bad" Christians who, for whatever reasons, did not follow the teachings of the Church, so left it, no matter what the cost.

Ministers found the first group very cooperative and did not have to work with the second group. The price which "good" Christians paid was perceived as part of the dues for being a member of the true Church; the price which "bad" Christians paid was viewed as their just desserts. In neither case was the price—which was often quite dear—addressed or negotiated.

Today, raw appeals to the Church and biblical authority are far less compelling for most Christians. While this may be celebrated or lamented, it is unarguably true. Even in a high school class, for example, if students ask why masturbation is viewed as a grave moral disorder, and the minister answers, "Because the Church and Bible say that it is," the discussion will have just begun. Twenty years ago, the discussion would have just ended. Therefore, while ministers must clearly know what the Church and the Bible teach, they will also need many more resources if they are to exert a moral influence on Christians today.

Today, a more ontological approach to morality is taking the place of the past, authoritarian one, at least on the pastoral level.

In other words, ministers must know not only what the Church teaches and understand why it is taught, they must also know and understand both the particular motives one may have for participating in a specific sexual behavior or relationship and the psychological, social, and spiritual effects of the behavior. In order to do this, ministers must possess a working knowledge of sexual issues and also must be able to discuss and transmit the knowledge in clear and credible ways.

Today, the line between who is a "good" Christian and who is a "bad" one is less clear. For example, some people may engage in masturbation, or participate in premarital sex, or be actively homosexual, and still attend Church regularly, be vibrant members of the Church community, and consider themselves to be "good" Christians. Others who religiously avoid any or all of the above behaviors may seldom attend Church, be invisible members of the Christian community, but still consider themselves to be "good" Christians. Ministers, therefore, while remaining faithful to their role, must be able to exercise great sensitivity, wisdom, and prudence with respect to how they present the moral values they represent.

Twenty years ago, ministers often may have paid short shrift to anyone who did not abide by official Church teachings regarding sexuality. Their attitude tended to be a Christianized version of "You're a bad apple, and we don't want you around here spoiling the bunch." Today, ministers must recognize that some Christians can violate some statutory teachings of the Church, yet remain Christian, and that other Christians can abide by all the statutory teachings of the Church, yet act in unchristian ways.

There is also a greater awareness today that whatever sexual behaviors a person participates in, there are always higher values to be considered. For example, a growing Christian sentiment today is reflected in Pope Paul VI's statement that "the teachings of Christ must ever be accompanied by patience and goodness, such as the Lord himself gave example of in dealing with people. Having come not to condemn but to save, he was indeed intransigent with evil, but merciful toward individuals."[1]

It is with these issues in mind that this chapter is written. The purpose of the chapter is to offer ministers a broader base for dialogue with respect to three sexual behaviors: masturbation, nonmarital sex, and homosexuality. Although these are not the only sexual behaviors that evoke moral concern, they are behaviors that ministers are often asked to address.

MASTURBATION

GENERAL INFORMATION

The word masturbation stems from two Latin words: *manu*, meaning hand, and *tubrare*, meaning to agitate. The following statistics indicate the extent and frequency with which people, at least in the United States, participate in masturbation:

- ninety-four percent of men and sixty-three percent of women report having masturbated at least once in their lives;
- eighty-six percent of unmarried men and sixty percent of unmarried women between the ages of eighteen and twenty-four masturbate, and ninety percent of unmarried men and eighty percent of unmarried women over the age of thirty masturbate;
- unmarried men between the ages of eighteen and twenty-four masturbate with a frequency of fifty-two times a year, and those over the age of thirty do so sixty times a year;
- seventy-two percent of married men over the age of thirty masturbate on an average of twenty-four times a year, and sixty-eight percent of married women over the age of thirty masturbate at a frequency of ten times a year;
- ninety-two percent of men who regularly attend church report masturbating compared to ninety-three percent of nonattendees, and fifty-one percent of women who regularly attend church report masturbating in contrast to seventy-five percent of women nonattendees.[2]

The fact that only one out of three people over the age of thirty-five and only one of six people under the age of thirty-five believe that masturbation is wrong indicates that past social and moral attitudes regarding masturbation have changed.[3]

MISCONCEPTIONS

No single sexual behavior has been more the subject of erroneous thinking than has masturbation. A myriad of fallacies surround it. For years, many people thought that masturbation caused physical and/or psychological harm. This misconception arose from the erroneous belief that semen possessed ingredients necessary for intelligence, strength, and one's overall welfare. When these ingredients left the system through masturbation, it was believed that the body became depleted, causing physical, intellectual, and moral damage. How female masturbation fitted into the picture is not clear.

This misconception caused overwhelming fear and anguish in many people and likely caused some problems by way of suggestion. This belief was generally accepted as true until the relatively recent present. In fact, in a 1957 study, fifty percent of graduating medical students and twenty percent of the faculty from five medical schools believed that masturbation caused physical and psychological problems.[4] Even as late as 1976, a study showed that fifteen percent of male and female medical students thought that masturbation could cause mental problems.[5] Unfortunately, this misconception is not extinct, even though there is much evidence indicating that masturbation, in itself, causes no physical or psychological harm.

Masturbation is fallaciously deemed a sign of immaturity (low self-esteem, sexual or social inadequacy, selfishness) or a sign of psychological pathology (compulsion, instability, schizophrenia, perversion, social or emotional conflicts, etc.). This misconception stemmed originally from the observation that many schizophrenics masturbate; in turn, that observation led to the erroneous conclusion that masturbation causes insanity. Using the same kind of faulty cause-and-effect reasoning, one could say that masturbation causes high intelligence because studies indicate that college-educated people masturbate significantly more than noncollege graduates.[6]

Contrary to the misconception, it has been shown that people who masturbate and those who do not show differences in self-esteem, sociability, or psychological adjustment. In fact, college students who masturbate tend to date more than those who do not masturbate.[7]

A third fallacy holds that masturbation is inherently habit-forming. Any behavior that affords pleasure and/or reduces anxiety can become compulsive; this includes jogging, eating, and even prayer. However, the mere fact that a person masturbates does not raise the issue of addiction. Masturbation *could* become habit-forming, but if it did, it would be less psychologically and physically damaging than many other habits, such as addictive eating, drinking, gambling, smoking, sleeping, and working.

Many people have been taught that masturbation prevents full psychosexual development. There has never been any evidence that this is true. People who masturbate can develop into fully mature adults. In fact, masturbation is often a part of normal psychosexual development. Thus, although it once was believed that masturbation could never be normal, harmless behavior, it is now known that most masturbatory behavior is not associated with any kind of psychological or physical anomaly.

By saying that most masturbation may be normal and healthy, however, we must not fall into another fallacy: namely, masturbation is always normal and healthy. There are very few, if any, behaviors that are always normal and healthy. When masturbation, or any other behavior, is used in any continuing way to escape reality, it is unhealthy. This topic will be dealt with in more detail in the following seciton on motives underlying masturbation.

In the same way, although masturbation does not preclude full psychosexual development, neither does masturbation guarantee it. In other words, it is also a misconception to think that people who do not masturbate are psychosexually immature. As with many behaviors, the more masturbation has become accepted as normal behavior, the more there is a tendency among some people to believe that those who do not engage in the behavior must have something wrong with them. Regarding this issue, no lesser authorities than Masters and Johnson write:

> People who have *never* masturbated, while in a statistical minority, should certainly not be made to feel abnormal. People who choose not to masturbate—whether or not they've tried it, whether or not their choice is based on religious conviction, personal preference, or some other consideration—have every right to that decision without any intellectual browbeating by self-proclaimed experts in sexual health. Sexual decisions, in the final analysis, must be personal.[8]

Another fallacy concerning masturbation is that it is a sign that a person should marry. Masturbation is never a sign that someone should marry, and when masturbation is compulsive, it is more likely to be a sign that a person should not marry until he or she discovers and solves the problem that is causing the compulsive behavior. Marriage is not a cure for compulsive masturbation any more than it is a cure for compulsive eating or drinking. A person who is compulsively masturbating before marriage is likely to masturbate compulsively after marriage.

Finally, ministers can recognize that many of the people they serve believe that masturbation and a fervent religious and prayer life are mutually exclusive. The problem with this misconception is that people who believe it think that they must choose between masturbation and God, and when they do masturbate, they may break off their relationship with God. This accounts for many adolescents and young adults pulling away from the Church at a time in their lives when they most need it. Since masturbation is such a common sexual experience, ministers must be aware that many people genuinely suffer under this last misconception. These people need the minister's careful concern to help them recognize that just as a spouse can love his or her partner and still masturbate, so, too, can people masturbate without breaking their loving relationship with God.

MOTIVES

People masturbate for many and diverse reasons, and masturbation affects their lives in different ways. In this section we will discuss these reasons and their effects from a psychological standpoint in order to help ministers better teach and pastorally counsel those involved in masturbatory behavior.

Masturbation is often used to reduce tension, just as drinking, eating, smoking, sleeping, taking tranquilizers, jogging, or soaking in a hot tub can reduce tension. From a psychological viewpoint, if the degree of tension a person experiences significantly interferes with his or her ability to function, and if the tension is not the result of failing to face a difficult situation, masturbation would ordinarily not be viewed as a source of concern. In fact, drinking alcoholic beverages, eating, smoking, sleeping, and taking tranquilizers to reduce tension would be sources of significantly more psychological and medical concern. Paradoxically, these latter tension-reducers rarely carry a moral connotation because they do not involve sexuality. If a person's tension is the result of not facing or handling reality well, and if masturbation is used to reduce tension instead of using the tension to motivate growth, ministers should help the person recognize that his or her masturbation could be a source of concern.

Often, masturbation is part of a fantasy sexual encounter, the theme of which is having a romantic sexual experience with someone. This motive is unlikely to be a concern if the person's fantasy is healthy, is a step in the direction of psychosexual development, motivates the person to grow in the direction of relating with another, demands insignificant amounts of time and energy, or in a married person, is directed toward one's spouse and does not replace sexual relations.

Masturbation would be a concern when the nature of the fantasy encounter is unhealthy (e.g., sadomasochistic), is regressive (e.g., sex with children), is a substitute for dating or relationships, demands significant amounts of time and energy, is a distraction from realities with which the person should be dealing, or in the case of a married person, is either frequently directed toward a person other than one's spouse or takes the place of sexual relations.

Sometimes the motive for masturbation is pleasure in the absence of other pleasures. A person's life may be relatively devoid of a reasonable and necessary amount of pleasure and joy; consequently, he or she masturbates as a means of experiencing at least some pleasure and distraction. Ordinarily, this would be a concern for two reasons. First, most people whose lives are devoid of pleasure and joy are responsible for this situation. Their fears and angers are preventing them from relating with people and experiencing the events that could give them pleasure and joy. The solution for this problem is not masturbation, but getting the help necessary to take hold of life and live it well. Second, as long as such a person continues to masturbate, he or she will unlikely feel the need to approach life in a more effective and, therefore, rewarding fashion.

The only time this motive would not be a concern is when a person is in a situation objectively devoid of pleasure or filled with pain: for example, a prison inmate, a shut-in, a soldier in combat, or a person in great physical distress.

Some people masturbate as a sign of rebellion and/or hopelessness. Masturbation can be a sign of silent rebellion in the same way that drug usage can be; namely, a behavior that countermands the dictates of one's parents and Church in a secretive way and, therefore, eludes responsibility and punishment. Ministers should recognize that this dynamic is often unconsciously present in the masturbatory behavior of many adolescents and young adults. It is a way of feeling good, establishing one's independence, and striking back at authority. As this person's feelings of anger and being controlled diminish, so also does the masturbation. This motive would ordinarily be looked upon with concern, because although emancipation and independence from parents, Church, and society could be steps in a healthy direction, rebellion is seldom a healthy step.

Masturbation can also be related to feelings of hopelessness. When some people feel hopeless, they experience an "eat, drink, and be merry, for tomorrow we die" attitude. They feel that things are so bad they have nothing to lose by masturbating, and it provides a chance to experience at least a litle pleasure. Hopelessness is rarely an appropriate response to reality and leads to no positive action. Consequently, people who masturbate for this reason need the minister's help in dealing with both their inner and outer realities in a more realistic, effective, and positive manner.

Sometimes the motive behind masturbation is compulsion. Some people feel absolutely compelled to masturbate. As we have seen earlier, any behavior that reduces anxiety and affords pleasure has addictive potential. When ministers encounter someone for whom masturbation is compulsive, they can realize that such behavior is likely to generate serious problems: it reduces or expends the tension that the person should be using as fuel for growth; it consumes a good deal of the person's time and energy; and in a man, it often causes a problem with premature ejaculation when he attempts sexual intercourse.

Ministers must understand two important points with respect to compulsive masturbation. First, the term "compulsive" is frequently misused when applied to masturbation. People who masturbate once or twice a day or even once a week have been classified as "compulsive masturbators." Especially in adolescence and young adulthood, masturbation would not be clinically considered compulsive unless it was beyond control and occurred three, four, or five times each day. Analogously, a person would not be classified as a compulsive eater if he or she ate a couple of meals a day or as a compulsive drinker if he or she had two cocktails each day.

The fact that the behavior is sexual does not change the situation. Therefore, ministers must be careful to use words that accurately describe the behaviors with which they are dealing, because inaccurate nomenclature can cause significant problems both for the people seeking help and for the professionals to whom the people may be referred.

Second, as a general rule, compulsive behavior is a symptom and indicates that the individual's underlying problems are of such magnitude as to require professional help. When this is the case, ministers' well-intentioned peptalks, moralizing, and scolding are more likely to add fuel to the fire than to extinguish it. The causes of any compulsive behavior are often unconscious, manifold, and require a good deal more expertise and time to uncover and deal with than does the average pastoral problem.

In summary, there is not necessarily one reason or motive underlying masturbation, any more than there is but a sole motive underlying any other behavior. Most behavior is multidetermined. Thus, ministers must be aware that there may be two or more issues involved in masturbatory behavior. Moreover, the effects of masturbation are not always the same for one individual, nor are they the same for all individuals. Depending upon the person's situation, some motives for, and effects of, masturbation are psychologically benign, while others are malignant.

PASTORAL IMPLICATIONS

Once ministers recognize the many motives and effects of masturbatory behavior, there are a variety of pastoral implications they must consider when addressing the issue of masturbation in an educational or counseling framework. First of all, the situation often arises in which a minister views masturbation as wrong, but the person the minister is teaching or counseling does not. A minister must use a good deal of discretion in such a situation. Telling a person that he or she is participating in immoral behavior when the person is convinced otherwise can create a great rift in the pastoral relationship. This could nullify whatever good the minister could do for the person in other areas of growth that are equally important, if not more important.

A minister who views masturbation as immoral can present his or her views in an informative and empathetic manner and invite the person to consider their merit and discuss them. To go beyond this is likely to result in a mutually frustrating and unhelpful experience. The situation to be avoided most is one in which people feel that as long as they masturbate, they will not be accepted by the minister.

Another situation that can arise is one in which a person views masturbation as being a seriously disordered behavior and feels negatively about himself or herself, but the minister does not view masturbation as wrong, or at least not as wrong as the person does. Again, the minister must exercise discretion. Telling a person that his or her behavior is not sufficient to evoke such terrible self-incrimination usually creates rather than reduces anxiety. The person's anxiety is caused by the feeling that the minister either is not being truthful in his or her attempts to be reassuring, is morally ignorant, or is not on the same wavelength as the person. Consequently, the person may feel that the minister is ineligible to offer true understanding.

In this situation—as in the first—the minister can share his or her own views on masturbation and invite the person to consider and discuss them. The minister must be careful not to hammer home his or her view. Doing so will likely cause unnecessary and counterproductive tension in the pastoral relationship.

If masturbation is a source of concern for a person, regardless of the moral factors, the minister can help the person explore its possible causes (some of which were mentioned in the previous section). This exploration should not be done like an auto mechanic poking around a car to see what is causing the problem. Rather, it should be done in a pastoral way, gently asking questions and reflecting on the answers in an interested but not overly intense manner.

When one or more possible causes of the person's masturbatory behavior are discovered, they can point the way to resolution: by assuring the person that his or her behavior is normal, or by helping the person change some patterns that may be causing or contributing to the behavior.

Ministers can also realize that while they may feel at home speaking of sexuality, it is likely that the person they are counseling is very sensitive about the issue and has mustered up courage over a period of time just to broach the topic with the minister. As one twenty-year-old responded to a minister who told her that she need not feel uncomfortable discussing masturbation,

"Okay, and when we're finished talking about me, let's comfortably talk about *your* masturbatory behavior."

Whatever a minister's view of the morality of masturbation, it is important to place masturbation in a proper perspective. The more masturbation is accented, the more the person being counseled defines himself or herself as "a masturbator." In addition, focusing on masturbation creates more tension, which likely leads to more masturbation, and which, in turn, can lead to despair and self-loathing. A person with a problem with masturbation probably spends one minute on masturbation to every five hours of other behaviors. Many of these other behaviors most likely contribute to being a good person and doing good things. The minister's focus, then, should not be on how to stop masturbating, but on how to help the person appreciate and increase his or her overall beauty. As the fabric of the person's life becomes fuller and more beautiful, the thread of masturbation becomes less and less noticeable.

Ministers must also be aware of a commonly held fallacy; namely, that if a person is sufficiently busy, has a good self-concept, and has rewarding relationships, he or she will not experience the need to masturbate. While the lack of these qualities of life can cause inordinate tension that a person may release through masturbation, it is not necessarily true that their presence will preclude masturbation. Genital contact can be extremely pleasurable, and some psychologically healthy people masturbate because they simply enjoy it and not because they are selfish, inverted, immature, or shallow. Undoubtedly, some ministers—as well as the people they counsel—will find this difficult to accept. Nevertheless, research and clinical experience indicate that this is true.

Finally, ministers must be keenly aware that people, especially young people, do not ordinarily approach ministers—or anyone else for that matter—with their questions and concerns about masturbation. Consequently, just as the minister initiates many other facets of religious education, so should the minister initate sex education as part of religious education. Not to mention masturbation and other forms of sexual behavior until they are brought up is to miss a rare opportunity to be of real psychological and spiritual help to people.

NONMARITAL SEXUAL BEHAVIOR

In the context of this chapter, nonmarital sexual behavior refers to having sexual intercourse when unmarried, whether or not with a future spouse.

GENERAL INFORMATION

Whatever a minister's view of nonmarital sex, people are engaging in it in significantly increasing numbers. As Rosen and Rosen state:

Survey research over the past ten years leaves little doubt that premarital intercourse has become normative and may become close to universal in the future. For some people, this trend is a rational and acceptable alternative to the standards of the past; for others, premarital sex brings fears of widespread promiscuity and moral decline.[9]

Without exception, the research since 1960 indicates that unmarried people are engaging in sexual intercourse earlier and in significantly larger numbers than in the previous twenty years. Typical of the research findings are the studies by Morton Hunt (1972) and Melvin Zelnick (1976). Hunt found that by age seventeen, approximately fifty percent of boys who later went to college and almost seventy-five percent who did not go to college had experienced nonmarital sex.[10] Zelnick found that over sixty-three percent of girls had experienced intercourse by age nineteen, the average age of first intercourse being approximately seventeen-and-a-half years of age.[11] Hunt also found, among married respondents, that ninety-five percent of eighteen- to twenty-four-year-old men and eighty-one percent of similarly-aged women reported having intercourse before they were married.[12]

The reasons for the striking increase in nonmarital sexual behavior over the past twenty year appear to lie in the following areas:

- Sexual mores have changed dramatically, so that young people view neither sexuality itself nor nonmarried sexuality in the same negative light as previous generations.
- Contraceptive devices are more reliable and easier to obtain.
- The age at which people are getting married has increased to 22.3 years of age for women and 24.8 years of age for men, thus making it less likely that people will wait until they get married to have sex.[13]
- There are significantly more single people in their twenties. From 1970 to 1981 the rate for unmarried women between the ages of twenty-five and twenty-nine more than doubled (from ten to twenty-two percent), and the rate for men in the same age range rose from nineteen to thirty-four percent.[14]

With regard to the relationships between religion and nonmarital sex, a study of women by Tavris and Sadd (1977) found that sixty-one percent of those who described themselves as "strongly religious" and seventy-eight percent of those who said they were "fairly religious" had experienced nonmarital sex.[15] Commenting on these results, Rosen and Rosen state:

Clearly, young women who believe strongly in religious prohibitions against sex but nevertheless are subject to strong peer pressure toward premarital sexual activity are placed in an awkward emotional position. Some may choose to ignore social pressure while maintaining their religious convictions, others may modify their religious beliefs to accommodate premarital sex. However, a large number probably live with the guilt and conflict produced by trying to combine two irreconcilable sets of standards.[16]

The fact that large percentages of young people are experiencing unmarried sex does not mean that they do not need a good deal of information, understanding, and help. As Morton Hunt states:

Many more young people are having premarital intercourse today than used to be the case, but this in itself does not tell us how genuinely liberated they are—how free from inner conflict about their own behavior, how unfettered and uninhibited in their sexual techniques, how capable of managing premarital coitus without doing physical or emotional harm to themselves or their partners.[17]

The fact that most of these young people have parents who could guide them through this challenging period does not diminish the minister's role as educator and counselor. Aaron Hass writes:

If a teenager asks a question, the most frequent response [from a parent] is, "What do you want to know that for?" They seem to think teenagers are super influenceable. That they want to know so they can run out and try it. We don't give teenagers enough credit. When they ask a question, what they're really expressing is their need to talk about sex.[18]

The fact that seventy-two percent of boys and seventy percent of girls reported that their parents do not talk freely about sex underscores this point.[19]

The sexual information gap left by parents *will* be filled. The question is, with what and by whom? Ministers are often in a good position to fill this gap, but only if they are viewed as approachable, understanding, and credible. The days have passed, however, when ministers can simply tell young people that nonmarital sex can, or will, damage them. In one study of college students, ninety-two percent of the men and ninety percent of the women felt that intercourse had enhanced their relationship, which had already been based on a deep mutual concern. Only 1.2 percent of the men and 5.4 percent of the women felt that it had been a damaging experience.[20] A similar finding in a study of college couples indicates that eighty percent said it was completely acceptable for couples who love each other to have intercourse, and twenty percent said that intercourse was acceptable between casual acquaintances.[21]

Although the subjects in both of the above studies were college students, there is nothing to indicate that many high school students and young people who do not attend college think or feel differently.

Hence, the challenge for ministers is clear. How can ministers properly educate young people with regard to nonmarital sex without presenting ideas that are in clear conflict with the young people's experiences? The following sections deal with the medical considerations (venereally transmitted diseases and pregnancy) and psychosocial considerations (motives for nonmarital sex) and pastoral implications of nonmarital sexual activity.

MEDICAL CONSIDERATIONS

The two chief medical considerations with regard to nonmarital sex are sexually transmitted diseases (STDs) and pregnancy.

Although there has been a good deal of effort expended on educating people about STDs, the number of people contracting STDs continues to increase rapidly. For example, from 1960 to 1980 gonorrhea increased in the fifteen- to nineteen-year-old age group by one hundred and forty percent and by one hundred and twenty percent among twenty- to twenty-four-year-olds. Over two million Americans contract gonorrhea each year, and it is estimated that over five million people in the United States have herpes, which is considered to be an epidemic proportion.[22]

The two basic reasons for the increased rates of STD are the increase of sexual activity with more than one partner, and gross ignorance about STDs. The ignorance stems largely from three fallacious beliefs, the first of which is that people always know when they have an STD; therefore, they will refrain from sex until the STD is cured. In fact, however, many people do not realize that they have an STD. For example, sixty percent of women and twenty percent of men who have gonorrhea do not have symptoms that they can detect.[23] Even people who do know that they have an STD often decline to tell their partners because they are ashamed or because they want to have sex, despite the likelihood of transmitting their STD. Also, some people with STDs do not refrain from sex because some STDs cannot be cured. For example, neither herpes nor acquired immune deficiency syndrome (AIDS) can be cured, at least at this time.

The increase in STDs may also be attributed to the fallacy that one must have sexual intercourse to contract STDs. The fact is that most STDs can be contracted through kissing, oral sex, or any mouth or genital contact with the infected area. Neither are there medications that one can take regularly—for example, penicillin or antibiotics—that will prevent STD. There is no medication that prevents STDs. Nor will washing with soap and hot water (after sexual encounters) get rid of STDs before they can enter the system. If this were true, not many people would have STDs.

Sadly, many people wrongly believe that once you contract an STD, you can not get one again. In fact, it is not uncommon that the same people are treated over and over again for an STD. Also, it is not always possible to tell if a person has an STD by examining his or her body, especially the genitals. Many STDs cannot be seen. Finally, too many people believe, "It can't happen to me because . . . " It is likely that every one of the many millions of people who have contracted STDs fervently believed this to be true.

It is not our intent to discuss STDs in any length; there are other very good sources of information. It is our intent, however, to help ministers become keenly aware of the threat and risk of contracting STDs when a person has sex with another person who is not a virgin. Race, age, educational level, or degree of religious devotion are not relevant factors with regard to contracting STDs.

Information about STDs need not be offered by ministers to those they teach or counsel as a scare tactic or as the main reason for avoiding nonmarital relationships. The information can be given in a matter-of-fact, informative way to help people understand that first, it is very possible that sooner or later a person who has nonmarital sex with a nonvirgin will contract an STD; and, second, while many STDs are easy to treat and cure, those that are left untreated for a period of time, those that are contracted by pregnant women, and those that are particularly virulous can cause damage that is serious, possibly long-term, and sometimes fatal.

The second medical consideration regarding nonmarital sex is pregnancy. The increase in nonmarital sex has resulted in a striking rise in teenage pregnancy, despite sex education courses and the easy availability of contraceptives. In fact, most adolescents do not use any contraception during their first intercourse experiences. One study reported that only thirty-two percent of middle- and late-adolescent subjects used birth control during their first intercourse, and only twenty-six percent of the subjects in early adolescence used any form of contraception.[24] Given these statistics, the following are points of information that young people—and those who minister to them—should know:

- almost one in five births is to a teenage mother;
- only one in five sexually active teenage women uses contraceptives consistently;
- among sexually active teenage women, seven in ten think they cannot get pregnant;
- children of teenagers have a death rate two to three times higher than children of mothers who were between twenty and twenty-four years old when they gave birth;
- the teenage mother faces a death risk sixty percent higher than that of mothers in their twenties;
- miscarriages, hemorrhages, anemia, and toxemia are more prevalent among teens.[25]

Still, unwanted pregnancies abound. Why? The reasons for a continuing high incidence of unwanted pregnancies are at least fourfold. First, the "it won't happen to me" defense is as strongly operative here as it is with venereal disease. Secondly, young people are often ignorant about contraception, because neither their parents nor their teachers made contraceptive information available to them. Thirdly, even when unmarried Catholic couples have at least a general knowledge of birth control, they are often disinclined to use it because of the Church's teaching. Hence, the irony evolves: the couple has nonmarital sex (which the Church teaches is wrong), but they do not use contraception (because the Church says it, too, is wrong). This is almost a foolproof way to become pregnant. Fourthly, young people (and sometimes older people) are ignorant about how one becomes pregnant. The most common mistake they make is the practice of interrupted coitus; that is, the male withdraws his penis from the female's vagina before he ejaculates. However, too many young couples are ignorant of the fact that the lubrication fluid that is often emitted from the penis before ejaculation also contains sperm which can impregnate the female.

When pregnancy outside of marriage occurs, the pregnant woman has the choice of four options which seldom, if ever, lead to a happy resolution.

The pregnant woman can choose to marry the father of the baby, a decision that may work out, but which is almost always regrettable. Generally, the people are not even close to being ready to marry, much less marry each other. And, often there is a deep and abiding level of—at least unconscious—resentment for having to marry and having to marry in a way that is fraught with secrecy, explanations, tension, and negative feelings from all sides.

The pregnant woman could choose to have the baby and keep it, but not marry. Many a young, pregnant woman makes such a decision at a time in life when she is in the midst of her own emotional and social growth. Her life will change radically, because her chief purpose in life suddenly becomes providing for her child while she is still a child herself.

The pregnant woman's third option is to choose to have an abortion. This decision can create significant psychological and moral problems. In many cases, the man does not want the woman to have the baby; hence, he exerts pressure on her to abort the baby, even though he may insist that the decision is hers and that he will support her, whatever she decides. In other cases, the woman also does not want the baby and has the abortion, only to protest later that she did not make a real decision because of pressure from the man or her family. The woman is then often left to agonize alone, because the relationship which led to her pregnancy has usually terminated by this time. With regard to the moral issue, the woman may experience conscious or unconscious feelings of guilt, which can cause depression, anxiety, and further self-damaging behavior.

A final option is that the woman can carry the baby to term and give it up for adoption. Although this may be objectively the most desirable option, it is not without its serious conflicts. Among them are the fact that "everyone" will know the woman is pregnant (and they will); her life will be significantly interfered with for at least a year during what may be a critical time of psychosocial development; and she may become emotionally attached to the baby before and during the birth and experience a good deal of ambivalence and guilt about giving the baby away.

In summary, STDs and unplanned pregnancies are real risks people take when they engage in nonmarital intercourse. Ministers should realize, however, that when dealing with young people, simply rattling off a list of facts about the medical dangers related to nonmarital sex is not educational. To give young people a truly educational experience, the minister should see to the following:

- Relevant facts should be presented in a clear and meaningful way.
- The educational process should be both intellectual and emotional.
- To help accomplish this, small group discussions and good films should be used.
- The process should include some personal thinking on the part of the young people themselves; for example, they can be assigned a short project on a particular subject to do on their own.
- The medical aspects of sex should not be isolated from the psychosocial and moral aspects. Risks should not be presented as cold, hard facts, but should be personalized; for example, ask: "When intercourse results in pregnancy, what has a couple done to the lives of three beautiful people (the boy, the girl, and the baby)?"
- It should not be implied that STDs or pregnancy are the only reasons for avoiding nonmarital sexual intercourse or that they represent trauma from which people never recover. Rather, STDs and pregnancy should be presented as real risks with po-

tentially serious consequences. Then young people can be helped to decide if they are willing and prepared to accept those consequences.

- Young people should be invited to talk privately with the minister, either alone or with a friend along for support. In such a situation, the minister can better tailor the educational experience to the individual and can build an emotional bond that will be a source of support.

PSYCHOLOGICAL MOTIVES

Understanding why a person behaves in a certain way can be as important as understanding the behavior itself. It is helpful to remember that unlike animal behavior, much human behavior is multidetermined. That is, more than one motive is operating at any one time. In the area of nonmarital sex, it is likely that two, four, or six motives can be operating at the same time.

Ministers must also realize that motives can be conscious or unconscious. Generally, people allow into their consciousness motives that fit their self-concept. This creates a difficulty: people can have moral certitude that their motives are pure and loving, when, in fact, they may be self-serving or destructive.

A motive that is dissonant with a person's self-concept can be disguised as a motive that is consonant. For example, it is unlikely that a young woman will declare, "I'm having sex with my boyfriend in order to hang on to him," even though that may be her predominant motive. She is more likely to assure herself and others, "I'm having sex because I love him," and to become terribly upset if the suggestion is made that she may also be trying to hold onto her boyfriend.

All of a person's motives, conscious and unconscious, influence behavior. That is why awareness of motives is so important. When people are confused by their behavior, or act in "stupid" ways, or say or do things they "don't mean," or forget things they "wanted" to remember, it is likely that motives are operative of which the person is unaware.

To help people be in a better position to make a decision with regard to engaging in nonmarital sex, ministers can point out that one or more of the following—and sometimes contrasting—motives can be present in nonmarital sexual relationships.

To demonstrate and communicate care, trust, compassion, fondness, and love is a positive motive for having sexual relations. All other factors being positive, it should lead to growth-producing and loving behavior. However, if all other factors are not positive, then the presence of this motive may not be sufficient to outweigh other relevant factors. This is the motive that most people claim when they engage in nonmarital sex. But young people often confuse any and all strong, positive feelings with love. Therefore, while this motive is often stated as being predominant, it also is the one that most disguises other less helpful and less healthy motives.

Ministers can help people who state that this is their main (and perhaps only) motive to look at the presence or absence of love in the other parts of their relationship. For example, ministers could help them address questions such as: "How often do I sacrifice, in a healthy way, my needs for his (hers)?" "How honest am I with him (her) with regard to what I like and dislike about his (her) behavior and our relationship?" "How willing would I be to let him (her) go if it became clear that this was in his (her) overall best interests?" "What would happen if he (she) did not want (or no longer wanted) sex until after we were married?"

Although not foolproof, honest answers to these questions can give people some insight into how much love is present in their relationship and how much of their deep feeling for each other is actually infatuation, romance, or sexual attraction.

Sometimes a person's motive for engaging in nonmarital sex is to prove his or her attractiveness and sexual competence. This motive consists of wanting to test or prove one's psychological or physical attractiveness, or one's ability to function well sexually. An important part of development through childhood, adolescence, and young adulthood is testing and proving oneself in a number of areas, sexuality being one of them. Sometimes, perhaps often, young people use sex as a proving ground or practice run. This may be understandable, but for the reasons discussed in the previous section, it is also risky.

The problem with this motive is that it does not prove what it sets out to prove. Some of the least attractive and least sexually adequate people in the world have sex every day, and the reason they do is that they are still trying to prove something that cannot be proven once and for all.

For some people, the motive for nonmarital sex is to exert power and control. Because sex is so gratifying and fulfilling to most people, it can be used as a powerful lever of manipulation. Acting on the same principle as the carrot-and-stick approach to motivation, a person can use sexual relationships to get what he or she wants and to keep his or her partner in place.

In dating, sex can be used to hold on to a person ("If I don't give him sex, he'll date someone who will"), to get what one wants ("If I have sex with her now when she wants it, I'll get her to type my term paper"), to feel important ("I'll make him demonstrate how much he needs me before we have sex"). When sex is consciously or unconsciously used to gain power or control, whatever is gained in the short run will be lost in the long run. Manipulation causes disrespect and resentment, which will eventually manifest themselves with a vengeance.

Sex can be used to express hostility. When used to demean the other person, sex can be used as a weapon. This can take various forms: making a person beg for sex, forcing a person to participate in demeaning sexual behaviors, causing a person to feel inadequate, and arousing a person and then refusing to have sex with him or her.

The problem with this motive is that one does not have a partner but a slave. If the "slave" remains in the relationship, he or she obviously has little self-esteem or social competence. This dynamic can end only with the persons despising themselves and each other.

Some couples have nonmarital sex to cure boredom. Not infrequently, after a few dates, there is not much for young people to discuss. Each person has a superficial knowledge of the other, yet the relationship has not developed to a point where either feels the need or has the ability to share on deeper psychological levels. Because sex is rarely boring, especially to young people, it fills the boredom gap nicely. Sex is more interesting than staring at the walls, and it is not as psychologically risky as being transparent and self-revelatory.

The problem with this motive is that the couple soon is communicating mostly about sex or with sex. Therefore, both the couple and the relationship become stunted. Even the sex eventually becomes boring, because only bodies are being shared devoid of intellects, emotions, and spirits.

Other couples have nonmarital sex to be "intimate" without being genuinely intimate. Many, if not all, developing people need to be touched by another in order to feel affirmed and important. When people cannot allow themselves to be touched psychologically because it's too threatening, they may allow themselves to be touched sexually.

The problem with this motive is the same that occurs when a person needs vitamin C but takes vitamin B because it is easier to get. Through the power of suggestion, the person may feel better temporarily, but sooner or later, he or she realizes that vitamins are not interchangeable. Being sexually intimate touches the body, but it does not in itself fill the soul; consequently, sex becomes an increasingly unsatisfactory and vacuous experience.

Some people use sex to feed an addiction. As is true with any behavior that both reduces tension and provides pleasure, sex has the potential of becoming addictive in the literal sense of the term. Sex addicts focus most of their energies on sex, can build up a tolerance so that more and different kinds of sex are needed, take great chances in order to have it, and experience withdrawal symptoms such as depression and anxiety when they go for periods without sex.

The problem with this motive is that the relationship between the sex addict and his or her partner is analogous to that between an alcoholic and his or her bartender. What appears at first glance to be a personal, perhaps even intimate, relationship is soon seen more accurately as a purely pragmatic one, a relationship devoid of any true concern, fondness, trust, or mutuality. It is a frantic, lonely relationship.

To escape from reality is another motive behind nonmarital sex. Because it can be temporarily all-absorbing, a sexual relationship can be an effective escape from the more anxiety-producing parts of reality. This especially pertains to young people who experience conflicts with parents, difficulties socializing with peers, and failures in school. The one oasis for them may be a sexual relationship, during which they can "forget" all their problems and feel affirmed or loved for a brief period of time.

The problem with this motive is twofold. First, the anxiety-producing parts of reality do not disappear. In fact, they reappear with a vengeance after sex because they have had more time to incubate. Secondly, because the relationship is used as an oasis, no meaningful growth can occur because growth entails confrontation, honesty, negotiation, compromise, and sacrifice, all of which create anxiety; and anxiety is not permitted on the oasis.

In summary, it is helpful for ministers to keep in mind that there are more possible negative motives than positive motives for nonmarital sexual relations (unfortunately, this is true of most behavior). Therefore, it is important that ministers walk the middle path between cynicism on the one hand, and naivete on the other. Moreover, ministers can be aware that both positive and negative motives can be present at the same time.

Ministers must also remember that they should be conversant both with the nature of motivation in sexuality and with some typical specific motives. In so doing, ministers will be in a better position to help people examine not only their dating and sexual relationships, but what these relationships and their attendant behaviors reflect about their overall life. Using this type of approach, ministers can open to people new vistas for self-understanding and growth that could well have lifelong, and possibly eternal, ramifications.

PASTORAL IMPLICATIONS

The topic of nonmarital sex is a very challenging one for ministers, because it is an area that is emotionally loaded, psychologically and socially complex, and morally debated. While pastoral prescriptions cannot be given in this or any other area of behavior, ministers do not have to throw their hands up in confusion or despair. The following thoughts are offered for consideration in an attempt to help ministers form a pastoral position and general plan with regard to teaching and counseling about nonmarital sex.

Above all, it is important that ministers be credible in this area so as not to be viewed as generally untrustworthy, especially by young people. Ministers are unlikely to be credible if they make global statements about nonmarital sex (which includes premarital sex) as being always seriously destructive to the people involved. People who have participated in nonmarital sex and who believe, correctly or incorrectly, that they have suffered no damage, or, in fact, believe that they have grown from the experience, will have a good deal of difficulty accepting such a generalization as valid.

It is also important that ministers realize that nonmarital sex can subjectively affect people in one of three ways: it can damage them to a mild, moderate, or severe degree; it can be a positive experience which is mildly, moderately, or very salutary; it can have virtually no effect on the people involved. The variables that influence the effects are the individual's perception of the rightness or wrongness of the behavior, the psychosocial-moral states of the individuals involved, the ages and maturity of the people, the nature and meaningfulness of the relationship, and the situation in which the behavior occurs.

As much as it might rankle some ministers, it is helpful to discuss nonmarital sex on levels that are more or less concrete, practical, and eminently sensible to young people. To use an analogy, a minister can play the role of a lamplighter who helps light the terrain so that people can see more clearly in which direction they are going. As lamplighters, ministers can ask people—directly or indirectly and in a variety of ways—illuminating questions which can brighten the darkness that surrounds nonmarital sex.

The first question one can ask is, "What are the chances that you could contract sexually transmitted diseases, become pregnant, or get someone pregnant while participating in nonmarital sex?" Those who respond that there is even a slight chance can be helped to explore their readiness and willingness to accept the consequences of these eventualities. People who respond that the chances are negligible can be invited to share the reasons for their belief and to examine their validity in the light of reality.

Another question ministers can ask is, "What are the chances that you could be psychologically and/or socially damaged as a result of participating in nonmarital sex?" This question allows ministers to touch upon an almost limitless number of issues, and it raises a great number of further questions pursuant to those issues:

- Are you being loved or being used?
- In the long run, are you doing a favor or a disfavor to your partner?
- Do you think your relationship will end happily or unhappily?
- What is the main adhesive in your relationship? Sex or a deeper motive?
- Does your sexual activity distract you from the *person* of your partner or from other important parts of your relationship?
- Is sex a source of mutual growth in honesty, autonomy, and freedom, or a source of regression manifested by selective honesty, overdependence, and possessiveness?
- If your relationship ends unpleasantly, how will having had sex affect the way you view yourself?
- Do you think sex will help you to see the reality of your relationship more objectively, or will it cloud your view?
- Do you think that the sexual part of your relationship can be kept confidential, or will it eventually get out to your peers, teachers, or parents?

- Does sex cause you to gravitate more and more to one another and to eschew other friends and interests?
- Will sex increase or decrease the possibility that you will learn new social skills in your relationship?
- If you end up marrying someone other than your present partner, will the sexual activity in which you are engaging cause you to feel positively or negatively about yourself?
- Does sex increase or decrease the possibility of developing overall sensitivity to your partner's needs?
- Will being in a sexual relationship make you feel open and honest or duplicitous and secretive in your relationships with your family and friends?
- Is there enough special about this relationship that it merits sharing the most intimate parts of your body?
- Does having sex add to, detract from, or not alter your relationship with God?

The responses to these questions can be discussed in light of their validity and what they mean in the context of the relationship and the individual's personal life.

A third question ministers can ask is, "What are the chances that you will be damaged spiritually by your sexual activity?" People who freely choose to listen to what a minister has to say about nonmarital sex are likely to be interested in the spiritual dimension of the issue.

People can be asked to consider what the chances are that sex will make them feel better or worse about themselves in their relationship with God. They need to discuss whether sex will motivate or demotivate them to pray and learn more about Jesus. People should also consider whether sex will allow religion to be important in their lives or will relegate it to the realm of "stupidity." Similarly, people need to question whether sex will allow them to feel like an integral part of the Christian community or cause them to feel apart or isolated from it. Finally, people should weigh seriously whether sex will cause them to feel like a virtuous person or an immoral one.

If ministers act as lamplighters, they have to accept the fact that some people wil find their light either too dim or too bright, and will choose to follow their own or someone else's light. In addition, some people may use the minister's light well, but end up taking a path which the minister would not take. In both these cases, the minister need not take a neutral stance when asked directions. The minister can offer directions which he or she feels are the most helpful, but still allow the person the freedom to accept or reject the directions without prejudice.

Finally, it is important for ministers to realize that illuminating questions will not always evoke meaningful insights, honest responses, or stimulating discussions. However, this general type of approach may prove more helpful than unhelpful. In fact, it is quite likely to be more helpful, or at least less damaging, than some traditional approaches which tend to ask and answer their own questions and dare anyone to disagree.

HOMOSEXUALITY

A sexual issue that is presently requiring and, in some cases, demanding the attention of both society and the Church is homosexuality. A person whose sexual orientation is homosexual is romantically and/or physically attracted to members of the same sex in an ongoing, rather than transient, fashion. This attraction may or may not be translated into overt behavior. Of the sexual behaviors discussed in this chapter, homosexuality generally creates the most anxiety in people. In fact, it is not uncommon for parents to state that they would rather see their children dead than see them become homosexuals.

GENERAL INFORMATION

Because increasing numbers of people, including ministers, are owning and communicating about their homosexuality, it is important that ministers have both an academic knowledge and an emotional understanding of homosexuality. Ministers should be able to relate with homosexuals in no less effective, accepting, or compassionate ways than they would with anyone else. If Christian ministry cannot successfully accomplish this, the Church will eventually be divided into a "gay Church" and a "straight Church," with a mutual antipathy that will infect the entire institution.

Statistics tell us that there are between five and ten million exclusively homosexual people in the United States and at least as many more who are bisexual. These statistics indicate that the chances are very good that ministers are dealing, and will be dealing, with homosexuals and bisexuals both in the ministry and in the general population. Consequently, it is important that ministers possess an adequate grasp of the current knowledge about homosexuality.

MISCONCEPTIONS

Unfortunately, it is not unusual for people who are highly intelligent and educated in other areas to be abysmally ignorant when it comes to the subject of homosexuality. As a result, they treat homosexuals, or allow homosexuals to be treated, in unchristian and unjust ways. To avoid becoming someone who engages in, or who fosters, such treatment, the minister can recognize some of the common misconceptions about homosexuality.

The first misconception about homosexuality is that its cause is known. In fact, the causes of homosexuality, bisexuality, and heterosexuality are unknown. At one time, it was believed that there was a strong hereditary factor in homosexuality, but the genetic theory of homosexuality has been generally discarded today.

There has been a fair amount of research with respect to hormonal factors and homosexuality, but the overall results have been contradictory and inconclusive. The general feeling in the scientific and medical communities at the present is that if hormones do affect one's sexual orientation, this may occur as a result of hormones affecting the brain during prenatal development. However, hormonal research is very complicated, and conclusive evidence, one way or the other, may not be available for a long time.

Most experts today tend to believe that even if a hereditary or hormonal predisposing factor were to be found, sexual orientation of any kind occurs largely after birth as a result of interactions with the environment, that is, with one's parents, siblings, peers, and other significant people. The specific nature of these interactions, however, is far from understood and unanimously agreed upon. For example, while some data suggest that a domineering mother and distant father may create an environment in which homosexuality may develop in males, other data indicate that there are many male homosexuals who did not have this parental combination and many male heterosexuals who did. As is the case with most behaviors, sexual orientation likely evolves from a combination of several factors, and there are likely several different paths to each sexual orientation.

It seems that the most realistic portrayal of the state of knowledge regarding the development of sexual orientation is described by Carol Offir: "It seems fair to say that at present we know as much about the development of human sexuality as, say, nineteenth-century physicists knew about subatomic particles—which is to say, not much."[26]

A second misconception contends that homosexuals do not like members of the opposite sex. It is true that *some* homosexuals do not like members of the opposite sex, but it is equally true that *some* heterosexuals do not like members of the opposite sex. Homosexuals can like and enjoy the company of both sexes equally, but be romantically and/or physically attracted only to people of the same sex, just as heterosexuals can like and enjoy both sexes equally but be romantically and/or physically attracted only to the opposite sex.

Another misconception holds that homosexuality is a matter of personal preference and choice. While the determinants of homosexuality are unknown, experts agree that both homosexual and heterosexual tracking is well on its way by five to seven years of age; and whatever psychological, social, and/or biological imprinting creates sexual orientation is completely beyond the control of the individual. To understand the fallacy of this position, heterosexuals can ask themselves, "When and how did I choose to become a heterosexual?" For this reason, the term "sexual preference" is a poor one because it connotes that people look over different sexual orientations and pick the one which they prefer. Ministers should be aware that this is not solely an academic point. A good deal of the moral condemnation of homosexuality has been based on the belief that homosexuals volitionally choose their orientation and could "unchoose" it if they so desired.

Some people believe that homosexuality manifests itself before twenty years of age. Although people acquire a homosexual orientation early in life, some may not become conscious of it until twenty, thirty, or fifty years of age. The same is true for heterosexuality. Some people with a heterosexual orientation do not become awakened to it until later in life.

In a society that is so heavily and emotionally heterosexual, it would not be rare for a person with a homosexual orientation to repress this orientation with its accompanying thoughts and feelings and attempt to adopt the heterosexual script of society. However, as the person's heterosexual attempts become increasingly frustrating and devoid of meaning, and society becomes more accepting of homosexuality, the person may get in touch with his or her homosexuality. This delayed evolution is particularly difficult if the person has married and has a family. Nevertheless, ministers can be aware that this situation is occurring with increasing frequency.

The misconception that tends to encourage unjust treatment of homosexuals is that which contends that homosexuals are psychologically disturbed. Whether or not homosexuality is in itself a psychological disorder is debated among professionals. A study that reviewed the relevant literature concluded that there are no psychological tests that can distinguish between homosexuals and heterosexuals and that there is no evidence of higher rates of psychological disturbance among homosexuals than among heterosexuals.[27] Unless one takes the position that homosexuals are psychologically disturbed by the very fact that they are homosexuals, and need not necessarily exhibit other signs of psychological disturbance, these data tend to indicate that homosexuals experience no more psychological disturbance than do heterosexuals.

Certainly there are psychologically disturbed homosexuals, some of whom flaunt their homosexuality in outrageous and hostile ways. But the same can be said of heterosexuals. Unfortunately, we do not have access to a representative sample of homosexuals—ministers, physicians, attorneys, laborers, psychotherapists, etc.—whom society at large considers to be responsible, mature, caring, holy, and good people. As a result, most people have a distorted picture of the homosexual's psychological and spiritual health.

That homosexuals are identifiable as homosexuals is an all too commonly held fallacy. In fact, only fifteen percent of men with extensive homosexual experience and five percent of women can be recognized as homosexuals by their outer appearance.[28] Homosexuals are no more identifiable as homosexuals than heterosexuals are identifiable as heterosexuals. One indication of this is how surprised people are when they learn that a relative, friend, or public personality is homosexual. By the same token, the same number of people are surprised when they learn that a family man (or woman) has left home to live with a same-sexed lover. There is a stereotypical homosexual, just as there is a stereotypical heterosexual. But relatively few people fit either stereotype. There are homosexual professional football players and heterosexual professional dancers.

A particularly malignant misconception contends that homosexuals are sexually attracted to children. This is an extraordinarily unjust presumption. Homosexuals can love children just as heterosexuals do, yet homosexuals are often suspect when they are around children. As a result, it is not unrare to find homosexuals deprived of jobs as teachers, youth workers, coaches, camp counselors, etc. In reality, the available evidence indicates that if a child is molested, the chances are eight out of ten that the molester will be heterosexual.[29]

Perhaps the most volatile issue with respect to homosexuality is the misconception that there is a consensus with respect to whether or not homosexuals can change their orientation. There are those who strongly believe that homosexuality, because it is virtually innate and/or is normal, cannot or should not be an area in which reorientation is attempted. These individuals believe that homosexuals who are comfortable with their orientation should be left alone, and those who are not should be helped to accept and adapt to it. On the opposite side of the issue are those who believe that all homosexuals, or at least those who are unhappy with their homosexuality, should be encouraged to change their orientation because it is maladaptive and damaging to them.

The controversy necessarily carries into a related area: Can homosexuals change as a result of psychotherapy? As would be expected, the answers differ according to one's attitude toward homosexuality.

There are some data that suggest that from thirty to sixty percent of homosexuals who seek reorientation therapy can become exclusively heterosexual. On the other hand, there are those who doubt the validity of those findings, either because the claims have not been validated by other researchers using the same methodologies, or because they believe that the subjects who were classified as homosexuals were actually heterosexuals with homosexual tendencies.[30]

A great deal of work must still be done in this area before this issue can be properly resolved. The one point that experts agree upon—and to which ministers should pay attention—is that homosexuals should *not* be forced into psychotherapy simply because of their homosexuality. Such treatment is unethical and would likely cause more harm than good.

Finally, many people erroneously believe that homosexual fantasies and experiences define a person as homosexual. In fact, homosexual fantasies and experiences are often a part of sexual development for people of both orientations. Many heterosexual adults have had homosexual fantasies and experiences as part of their childhood, adolescence, and even adulthood. This is especially true when young people are living in a closely knit, same-sexed environment; for example, a boarding school, a seminary, a convent, the military (especially in isolated situations), or prison.

At least one million wives and two to three million husbands have homosexual experiences outside of marriage while considering themselves to be completely or primarily heterosexual.[31] By the same token, homosexuals can have heterosexual fantasies and experiences (including heterosexual marriage), but remain essentially homosexual.

The hope is that people in general and ministers in particular will realize that homosexuals are basically and generally the same as heterosexuals, except for one part of their personality. With the exception of that part, homosexuals are no more alike than are heterosexuals. At the same time, homosexuals experience the same kinds of needs, fears, hurts, aspirations, problems, gifts, and values as heterosexuals.

Pastoral Implications

Recognizing and dealing with the misconceptions surrounding homosexuality are the first steps ministers must take before entering a pastoral relationship with a homosexual or a person with homosexual tendencies. For that relationship to be helpful, however, there are certain pastoral implications ministers would do well to consider.

Ministers can realize that most, if not all, homosexuals who were raised in the Christian tradition learned that homosexuals are psychological and moral lepers. No other segment of society—including racial minorities, physically or psychologically disabled people, or criminals (including murderers)—has had a similar experience.

While other minorities have experienced rejection by society, they are welcomed by their families, friends, and Church. Homosexuals, however, are not only rejected by employers, society, and the Church, they are often rejected by their closest relatives and friends, and frequently they even reject themselves. It is virtually impossible for a heterosexual to approximate what this feels like. Therefore, it is important that heterosexual ministers do not gloss over this very important issue. Consequently, when people bring the issue of their homosexuality to a minister, it means

- They have developed either a great deal of trust in the minister or have reached a crisis point in relation to their homosexuality. In either case, this is information of which the minister can be aware.
- They are very frightened because they are risking a great deal in sharing the information. Sometimes, they will cover up their fear or cover it over with a facade of bravado or hostility. In either case, the minister need not be misled and can be sensitive to what the person is really feeling.
- They are expecting to hear the antihomosexual tape that the Church has played so long and clearly. Therefore, they will be acutely sensitive to any signs of shock, repulsion, and rejection; and they may see these signs even when they are not present.
- They may return frequently for help because the minister seems to be the only person who truly understands, or they may never return because they correctly or incorrectly picked up negative reactions from the minister, found the revelation too threatening, or received the help they needed.

Ministers must be keenly aware of their own attitudes and feelings toward homosexuality and homosexuals. It is likely that many ministers have been indoctrinated with antihomosexual tapes and, at least on some deep level, are influenced by them. Instead of denying biases and fears regarding homosexuality, it is more helpful to admit them, be aware of them, understand them, and work with them.

One of the reasons, perhaps the strongest reason, that homosexuality evokes intense emotional responses is that many people are fearful that they are, or could become, homosexual. This is understandable because sexuality is often not a clearly defined entity. When dealing with homosexuality, many people, including ministers, find that frightening questions arise: "What if I am a latent homosexual? What if relating with this person triggers some homosexual feelings in me? What if people will think I'm a homosexual because I have a relationship with this person? What if he (she) wants our relationship to develop into an intimate relationship?" Dealing with these issues within oneself, and when helpful, with colleagues, can be a good and necessary step in the direction of being helpful.

It is important that ministers recognize that homosexuality (like heterosexuality) is an important part of a person's *identity*. Homosexuality is not simply a habit of which one may approve or disapprove. Hence, the old chestnut "Hate the sin, but love the sinner" runs into trouble in a minister who views homosexuality as seriously immoral and sinful.

One may reject alcoholic behavior, for example, but accept or even love the *person* who is the alcoholic. This can occur because alcoholism is not an essential part of the person; it is a disorder that can be treated. But to reject homosexuality is to reject the *person*. Heterosexuals can imagine how they would relate to a minister who directly or indirectly communicated, "I reject your heterosexuality and heterosexual behavior, but I accept you."

Of course, distinctions are made between a homosexual orientation and homosexual behavior. However valid this distinction is, it raises a difficult question. For example, if an orientation, that is, a tendency toward a specific behavior (e.g., homosexuality), is acceptable, how can all behavior that naturally flows from it be automatically gravely immoral? Perhaps an illustration will elucidate the problems raised by this question. If a man has a heterosexual orientation and rapes a woman, society says that the heterosexual orientation is an acceptable one but that the *specific* behavior that arises out of it is disordered. With a homosexual orientation, however, *all* behavior that naturally flows from it is considered to be disordered. There seems to be no other *acceptable* psychosocial orientation from which all consequent behaviors are judged to be *unacceptable*.

In reality, can a minister who loathes homosexual behavior ac-

cept the homosexual person, even if the person does not participate in sexual behavior? Whatever discrete distinctions philos-
ophers and theologians may make, it seems that ministers who
view homosexual behavior as inherently wrong, abnormal, or
sinful are going to experience great difficulty communicating acceptance and love to a homosexual, whether or not he or she is
participating in sexual behavior.

While a minister may not believe that all homosexual behavior
is wrong, abnormal, or sinful, he or she does not have to believe
that all homosexual behavior is right, normal, and moral. Just as
heterosexuals can participate in destructive sexual behavior, so
also can homosexuals. Any sexual behavior, regardless of whether it is homosexual or heterosexual, that places the self-esteem,
integrity, freedom, trust, or health of people in jeopardy is destructive, and therefore immoral. Whether or not it is subjectively sinful depends upon other elements.

When a homosexual brings a problem to a minister, it is helpful for the minister to understand the place that the person's homosexuality plays in his or her problem. Some believe that all
problems that a homosexual could have stem from his or her homosexuality. There are others who would never view homosexuality as a contributing cause to a person's problem. Neither position is universally valid. Each individual is unique. For one
man, his homosexuality may have absolutely nothing to do with
his depression, and for another, his depression may be directly
related with being a homosexual. For one woman, her sense of
loneliness and isolation may in no way be connected with her
homosexuality, whereas for another woman, her homosexuality,
or at least her perception of her homosexuality, may be a significant contributing cause.

Ministers cannot always take as valid the person's estimate as
to the place of homosexuality in his or her problems. A man may
use his homosexuality as an excuse for mismanaging his life, a
life he would mismanage if he were heterosexual. A woman may
insist that she has worked through her lesbianism, whereas, on
an emotional level, she has not even begun to address it.

Ministers who are, themselves, homosexual can be aware that they may face similar tensions when working with same-sexed people as heterosexual ministers face when dealing with other-sexed people. They may find some same-sexed people very attractive physically and/or psychologically and be drawn to them. Whatever a minister's sexual orientation, he or she must be aware that when teachers and counselors become emotionally and/or physically involved with those they teach and counsel, they can no longer function as helpers and may, in fact, leave the person more damaged than when he or she sought help.

In moral pastoral situations it is often the parents of a homosexual son or daughter who will seek the aid of a minister. This usually occurs when the parents first find out that their child is homosexual, a discovery that can create a great deal of emotional upheaval. The reasons for the upheaval are several. The parents, directly or indirectly, consciously or unconsciously, blame themselves and/or each other, believing that they failed their child in some way. They are anxious about what other people will think and say. They are worried as to what it will mean to the family constellation and their future relationship with their son or daughter. They are disappointed that they may not have weddings, births, and grandchildren. They are anxious as to how they will react to their son's or daughter's partners. They are concerned about their child's psychological and physical welfare. They wonder who can help their child, and they react with antagonism when their son or daughter relates that no help is needed.

Ministers need first to allow the parents to "decompress," that is, to get out their fears, angers, hurts, confusions, and questions. Sometimes it is more helpful for ministers to meet first with the parents apart from their son or daughter, thus freeing the parents to be candid and spontaneous, without risking damage to their son or daughter.

The minister's main role is to help the parents communicate and clarify their thoughts and feelings and to assure them that their reactions are natural and to be expected. Often parents will ask the minister questions, some of which can be answered ("Will you see Jim if he agrees to talk with you?") and most of which cannot be answered ("What part did we play in all of this?").

Gradually, the minister can attempt to help the parents grow from the understandable, but less than helpful, stages of shock, anger, blame, self-pity, and confusion to a more helpful reaffirmation of their son or daughter, so that together they can face the future in a spirit of mutual understanding and support.

Besides dealing with homosexuals themselves, ministers have a responsibility to educate other Christians with regard to homosexuality. Much of the prejudice that exists toward homosexuals is based on erroneous information of the kinds discussed earlier. This misinformation can be corrected by ministers in an effort to weaken the bases of prejudice. Ministers can also help Christian people understand that there is nothing in Christianity that permits prejudice or mistreatment of anyone, homosexual or otherwise. Because there is a large segment of Christianity that disapproves of homosexuality, ministers can help people recognize the differences between disapproval and actively interfering with the civil, social, and moral rights of homosexuals as human beings and as Christians.

The Church has gradually become aware both of the injustices perpetrated on homosexuals due to prejudice and of the responsibility of Christians in the face of these prejudices. As one group of ministers directs its members:

... the grammar schools and religious education programs in the Archdiocese should make efforts to foster in their students a full and deep respect for the human and civil rights of homosexual persons. Prejudicial attitudes are developed all too young in our society, and we have an obligation to work against intolerance at all ages. Thus teachers should be careful to deal effectively in their classes with any overt incidents of homophobia; and in teaching about the nature of Christian community, they should endeavor to promote respect for and acceptance of people of all sexual orientations.[32]

These words are well worth the attention and living out of all Christian ministers.

GENERAL MORAL CONSIDERATIONS

Typically, when people bring sexual difficulties, conflicts, or confusions to a minister, the subject of the rightfulness or wrongfulness of their behavior arises. A minister whose moral theology is traditional may respond with some version of, "The Church teaches that this behavior constitutes a grave moral disorder and presumes that anyone who participates in it is guilty of serious sin." A minister whose theology is revisionist may respond with some variation of, "Most contemporary moralists believe that, to judge a behavior accurately, not only the act itself, but the circumstances surrounding it must be taken into account in order to make a valid moral judgment." There may be a time and place where these responses could be appropriate and helpful, but in most instances they would be unhelpful.

Analogously, the parent who answers, "Sixty," to her child's question, "What does five times twelve equal?" is meeting the child's superficial need, but missing the child's deeper need and problem; namely, the child lacks the knowledge, ability, or confidence to go through the mathematical process by himself in order to arrive at an answer. So, too, it is unlikely that many people seeking help from a minister are truly helped by only being told what the Church teaches or what contemporary theologians are saying about a moral issue. Therefore, whatever a minister's moral theology, there are some issues that may be helpful to consider when working on the pastoral level.

THE MORAL ORDER AND THE PASTORAL LEVEL

It is generally accepted that there is a difference between the moral order and the pastoral level. The moral order deals with the way things should be, while the pastoral level deals with the way things often are. Both are important. Without moral criteria, ministers would be forced to work within a diluted and illusive Christian framework; without a pastoral approach, the minister's role would be solely that of moral commentator and referee.

Unfortunately, the role of moral referee is a tempting one for at least three reasons. First, it is a good deal easier, just as it's easier for a baseball umpire to call a player "out" than it is for a coach to help the player avoid being called "out." Second, most ministers have spent the greater part of their lives being morally judged; therefore, a judgmental response is likely to be more reflexive and enduring than an accepting, empathetic one. Third, even though there can be confusion on the moral level, it is far more clear ("The Church teaches . . . ") than the pastoral level ("Oh, brother, what do I do now?"). Ministers can be aware, however, that there seems to be an inverse relationship between judging and helping. As Richard McCormick points out: "The basic problem with moralism is that it bypasses and therefore effectively subverts the process leading to understanding."[33] Without genuine understanding and empathy, there is no pastoral help.

Thus, effective ministers combine the two dimensions (moral order and pastoral order) by employing some variation of the approach that says, "Let's try to envision what kinds of behavior will allow you to relate with yourself, others, and God with a maximum degree of love, justice, integrity, and freedom (the moral order). Then we'll see how, why, and where there is a distance between where you'd like to be and where you are now, and try to discover how we can close the gap (the pastoral level)."

APPLYING THE MORAL ORDER

It is generally accepted that there is a difference between the objective moral order and its subjective application.

The objective moral order is based on the belief that basic Christian values of love, justice, honesty, and spiritual awareness should permeate all behaviors. From this belief have evolved specific moral principles and laws with respect to specific behaviors. However, recognizing the imperfection of human nature, Christian tradition teaches that situations may arise which reduce the degree of subjective responsibility or culpability. For example, the Catholic Church's *Declaration on Certain Questions Regarding Sexual Ethics* states:

It is true that in sins of the sexual order, in view of their kind and cause, it more easily happens that free consent is not fully given; this is a fact which calls for caution in all judgments as to the subject's responsibility.[34]

This general attitude also applies to specific sexual behaviors. For example, the same document also states:

On the subject of masturbation modern psychology provides much valid and useful information for formulating a more equitable judgment on moral responsibility and for orienting pastoral action. Psychology helps one to see how the immaturity of adolescence (which can sometimes persist after that age), psychological imbalance or habit can influence behavior, diminishing the deliberate character of the act and bringing about a situation whereby subjectively there may not always be serious fault.[35]

At the same time, however, Christian tradition also teaches that no sexual behavior it defines as objectively immoral can ever be permitted, no matter what the circumstances. Many contemporary moralists take issue with this point. They believe that if the injunction against killing can admit of exception (as in the case of a just war or capital punishment), then it would seem reasonable to expect that a particular set of circumstances could arise in which a single sexual fantasy, an act of masturbation, premarital sex, or homosexuality could be permitted. This would be especially true if not participating in the behavior would cause a greater violation of the values that the law was meant to protect than would refraining from participating in it.

One of the foundations for this position is found in the writings of Thomas Aquinas, who taught that truth and rectitude embodied in general moral principles and laws apply to the majority of cases but may fail in some specific situations. Aquinas gives the following example of such a principle: On the basis of reason, goods entrusted to another should be restored to the owner. He demonstrates, however, that when this general principle is applied to a particular situation (e.g., if the goods are reclaimed in order to fight against one's country), it would be morally permissible not to return the goods to the owner. In other words, it would be good to violate the general principle. Aquinas then states, " . . . the greater the number of conditions, the greater number of ways in which the principle may fail. . . . "[36]

In summary, at whatever point on the scale beginning with the formal teachings of the Church and ending with the revised teachings of the theologians that ministers fall, they should have sound methodological reasons for choosing that point. It is not enough simply to have landed there as a result of blind obedience ("If the Church teaches it, you'd better believe it") on the one hand, or moral anarchy ("People should be allowed to do what they want") on the other.

RIGHT OR WRONG: WHO IS THE JUDGE?

It is generally agreed upon that, in the last analysis, it is the individual and his or her conscience that is responsible for judging the rightfulness or wrongfulness of an act.

The Church has the right and the responsibility to teach the moral precepts of any behavior, including sexual behavior. Ministers also have the right and responsibility to reflect these teachings in a pastorally helpful manner. But an authentic moral decision and judgment cannot be made until the individual does his or her best to develop a deep understanding of the relationship between the moral law and his or her own unique being and situation.

While there is no set recipe that will cause this to happen in a pastoral relationship, it may prove helpful to answer and discuss some version of the following questions:

• What are your deepest intentions and motives, and are they basically selfish, altruistic, or destructive?
• Are you maximizing the freedom you have to act in the most Christian ways possible?
• Are you making concerted efforts to grow in the moral area, and are you making some progress, however gradual it may be?

- What are the short-term and long-term consequences of your behaviors, and are they more apt to increase or decrease love in your life?
- Given that you are faced with a "lesser of evils" moral choice, in which direction does your greater duty lie?
- Given that you are faced with a seemingly unresolvable moral conflict, which decision does your deepest and most honest sense tell you is probably the correct one?
- What are the unique factors in the context of who you are and the situation you are in that should be considered in making a moral decision?
- Will your behavior bring you closer to others, make it easier to withdraw from others, or have virtually no effect on your relationships with others?
- Do you have as full an intellectual, affective, and spiritual understanding of the issues involved as possible, or is your awareness avoidably superficial?
- Have you given serious consideration to what the Church and theologians have taught regarding the issues with which you are concerned?
- Will your behavior improve, impair, or have no effect on your spiritual life?

The moral discernment process includes helping people ask, consider, and answer these questions as fully and honestly as possible.

Regarding conscience, effective ministers can recognize that through the ages conscience has been more or less typically viewed as a tablet that was mostly blank, except for the imprinting of "the natural law." It was the duty of the Church to "inform" an individual's conscience, that is, to write upon the tablet both moral problems and their solutions. The end result was considered to be a "properly formed conscience." Although this notion is still present in some quarters, it is gradually being replaced by the view that conscience, like any human dimension, is personal, developmental, integral, and social.

Describing conscience as "personal" means that two individuals could be faced with the same moral dilemma, but choose to solve it in qualitatively different ways; the possible result being that each individual makes a morally responsible decision. This view is in contrast to conscience being viewed as "collective," which means that there would be only one responsible way to solve a moral problem. Thus, if two people chose to solve the same problem differently, one would necessarily have made a morally irresponsible decision.

"Developmental" means that a conscience is, or should be, always evolving and growing. Thus, a moral decision made three years ago may be qualitatively different than one made today, but both could be morally responsible decisions, given the differing levels of development.[37]

"Integral" means that a conscience is influenced by and influences the body, intellect, emotions, and spirit. A conscience does not work independently or in isolation. Hence, every moral decision-making process includes, for better or for worse, the functioning of the central nervous system, the autonomic nervous system, and the spiritual system. Moreover, the nature, functioning, and experiences of one system are not viewed as superior to any other.

This is in contrast to the older notion that the intellect and the spirit are superior to the physical and psychosocial needs and emotions of an individual. Thus it was thought that moral decisions should be made at these "higher levels." Information from other levels was to be virtually ignored, because it would contaminate the decision process. However, when this view is put into action, a dualism results, the behavioral effects of which can fragment the individual in destructive ways.

"Social" means that what is morally good for the individual must be weighed against what is morally good for others and society at large. This is in contrast to the older principle that what is morally good for the individual is, by necessity, morally good for everyone in the individual's life, as well as for society and the world at large.

With an enlightened understanding of conscience, things are

much more complex and difficult than they once were. The older understanding of conscience formation was a relatively simple procedure. The minister informed the individual what was morally good and what was morally evil, and the person chose one over the other. The entire process could, and often did, take only five or ten minutes. However, as conscience is now understood, a melange of variables must be considered, weighed, and balanced: a process similar to solving a complex calculus problem. Depending upon the nature of the issue, the individual, and the number of poeple involved in the situation, this process could take a person five minutes, five months, or longer to arrive at a responsible moral decision.

Do Not Lose God

Great care should be taken that God does not become lost in our concern about morality in general, and sexual morality in particular. It is not uncommon that God gets lost in the dust stirred up by family feuds between traditionalists and revisionists, deontologists and teleologists, absolutists and contextualists, intrinsicists and proportionalists, moralists and ethicists, theologians and empirical scientists, etc.

If ministers are not continually cautious, God can become irrelevant in moral teaching and counseling. Even worse, God can be presented as an ogre. As Daniel McGuire writes:

. . . God [can be] put in the position of vindictively allocating massive retaliation for sexual acts many of which do no perceptible harm. In the eyes of sensitive people, this could only make the God of Love into a God of atrocity.[38]

It is critically important that God and a positive image of God be present in every discussion—academic or pastoral—regarding sex.

Ministers can also be mindful that God is reflected both in their demeanor and in the content of what they teach and counsel about sex. To keep themselves aware of this important fact, ministers can ask themselves:

- When I speak of sex in relation to God, do I portray an unconditionally loving and compassionate God or a God with whom no sensible person would want to spend a weekend, much less an eternity?
- Do I describe sex as an inherently beautiful and precious gift from God, or basically as a curse from God before marriage and a duty and responsibility after marriage?
- Do I portray God as THE JUDGE of the morality of all behaviors, or as sort of a court bailiff who frees people or takes them into custody on the orders of the Church and clergy?

An unconditionally loving God should always be the central focus of any discussion of Christian morality, with God's justice and mercy seen as direct manifestations of that love. Moreover, it is important to keep in mind that ministers are viewed as the direct ambassadors of God. Therefore, a minister's demeanor, attitudes, and statements will, consciously or unconsciously, affect each individual's perception of God.

In summary, ministers must be able to walk the line between being morally preoccupied and morally disinterested. Andre Guindon addresses this point when he writes:

There are very few good moral counsellors—for the "good" reason that very few people know what morality is all about. Many who, because of their function, have assumed the role of moral counsellor are often tempted either to play God, by distributing already-made judgments on the interior state of their clients, or shy away from their role and sometimes indulge in amateurish psychotherapy.[39]

Of course, the more that ministers are sensitive to, appreciative of, and comfortable with their own sexuality, the more psychologically and morally facilitative they will be.

5. The Personally Reflective Minister

To be pastorally effective, ministers must be personally reflective. Some ministers are personally unreflective; that is, they virtually never examine their psycho-spiritual state and effectiveness, causing them to remain stunted. Other ministers are personally hyperreflective; that is, they spend inordinate amounts of time and energy examining themselves and their effectiveness, to the extent that they lose their balance. Still other ministers are healthily reflective; they keep one eye on themselves and one eye on others in order to maintain a healthy equilibrium.

The first section of this chapter will deal with ministers reflecting on themselves and their work in the local Church so that they can learn more about which behaviors are helpful and which are unhelpful to themselves and others. In this section, ministers are invited to fill out a self-report questionnaire that deals with the psychological, social, ministerial, and spiritual dimensions of the minister's life. The section also includes an example of an evaluative instrument that can be used to assess the effectiveness of a parish's structure and function.

The chapter's second section offers ministers a series of brief meditations. Ministers are encouraged to use these meditations to facilitate their own reflections and self-evaluation. The chapter's final section sums up the chapter and calls ministers to seek clear evaluative information on themselves so as to grow in their service of others.

EVALUATION IN MINISTRY

Without evaluation, it is too easy for ministers, or any professionals, to fool themselves into thinking that they are doing a better or a worse job than they actually are. Some ministers never evaluate themselves or allow themselves to be evaluated. Others do informal evaluations which lead them to the conclusion that things are going pretty well or not so well. However, concepts such as "things," "pretty well," and "not so well" are useless with regard to a clear and helpful assessment of one's effectiveness. It is necessary to concretize "things" into specific behaviors and events, and to specify how well is "pretty well" and how poorly is "not so well."

What follows in this section are samples both of a self-evaluation form for ministers and of an evaluative questionnaire which can be completed by parishioners or by any other people ministers may serve.

SELF-EVALUATION FOR MINISTERS

Directions: This self-evaluation consists of four main sections: psychological, social, ministerial, and spiritual. Each section has twenty-five statements that you can evaluate in terms of the following levels of satisfaction:

A. I am very satisfied (which does not mean that there is no room for continual growth).

B. I am satisfied (which means the area is not a problem to you but, on the other hand, you don't feel it's as good as you'd like it to be).

C. I am dissatisfied (which means that, in all honesty, you feel that things could be significantly better in this area).

D. I am very dissatisfied (which means that a good deal of improvement is needed in this area).

After you consider each item, write the appropriate letter in the blank space. For example, if you are relatively satisfied with the amount of leisure time you take, you would place a B in the blank before the item; if you are dissatisfied, you would place a C in the blank.

You may approach this evaluation any way you wish; however,

it is suggested that you do one part at a time (that is, do one segment today, another tomorrow, and so on) in order to concentrate fully and to digest each part. The entire form should not take more than forty-five minutes to an hour to complete.

Part I: Psychological Life

___ 1. with the amount of recreational time I take for myself.

___ 2. with the degree of freedom I have in making decisions that significantly affect my welfare.

___ 3. with the confidence I have in my ideas and emotions and my willingness to communicate them.

___ 4. with my ability to be honest with myself with respect to my motives, needs, doubts, insecurities, and values.

___ 5. with my overall self-image (intelligence, appearance, acceptability).

___ 6. with the degree of self-discipline I exercise.

___ 7. with my ability to recognize and accept my imperfections, weaknesses, and mistakes.

___ 8. with my general sense of peace, fulfillment, and happiness.

___ 9. with my levels of energy, motivation, and enthusiasm.

___10. with the degree to which I am actualizing my potential.

___11. with my ability to handle stress (frustration, conflict, pressure) in a constructive manner.

___12. with the balance between my intellect and emotions.

___13. with my sexuality (orientation, expression, fulfillment).

___14. with how well I have allowed past hurts to heal.

___15. with how well I have forgiven myself my worst transgressions.

___16. with the ease with which I allow myself to experience affection, compassion, fear, anger, loneliness, guilt, hurt.

___17. with my ability to be vulnerable and not always in control.

___18. with my ability to be alone and to enjoy and use solitude.

___19. with my ability to leave relationships and situations when they become destructive.

___ 20. with my ability to accept responsibility for my happiness, my decisions, my mistakes, my life.

___ 21. with the degree to which I have psychologically emancipated myself from my family so that I am my own person.

___ 22. with the degree to which I can own my prejudices and work to overcome them.

___ 23. with my ability to know well my demons (laziness, pride, greed, pleasure, lust, hostility, jealousy, competitiveness, power, self-destructiveness) and to predict in what situations they will attempt to wrest control.

___ 24. with my ability to appreciate my gifts fully and to use them without embarrassment or apology.

___ 25. with my ability to relax with myself and not have to prove to myself that I am attractive, intelligent, carefree, strong, sexual, superior, humorous, or profound.

Part II: Social Life

___ 1. with the way I view people in general (as generally kind, trustworthy, well-intentioned, hurtful, selfish, manipulative).

___ 2. with the number of good friends I have and the amount of time I spend with them.

___ 3. with the amount of time I spend socializing with other ministers.

___ 4. with the number and quality of relationships I have with nonministers.

___ 5. with the way I allow and encourage others to be critical of me.

___ 6. with my ability to say no to people when it is appropriate.

___ 7. with my ability to be absolutely, yet constructively, honest with all people.

___ 8. with the degree that I am natural, relaxed, unguarded, and unpretentious around people.

___ 9. with the degree to which people feel that they can discuss embarrassing issues with me.

___ 10. with my ability to demonstrate compassion, affection, joy, hurt, fear, and anger to people.

___ 11. with my ability both to give *and* to receive affection.

___ 12. with the degree to which I am punctual, reliable, and consistent in my relationships with people.

___ 13. with my ability to work like a team member, needing neither to lead nor to follow when one or the other is unhelpful.

___ 14. with my ability to apologize to people when it is appropriate and helpful.

___ 15. with my ability to confront people when it is appropriate and helpful.

___ 16. with my ability to tolerate people who are different or abrasive.

___ 17. with my relationships with both men and women.

___ 18. with my ability to relate well with all kinds of people of all ages.

___ 19. with my sensitivity to the areas of insecurity and vulnerability in others.

___ 20. with my ability to relate with others without needing to impress, control, entertain, judge, or scold them.

___ 21. with my ability to perceive and relate with authority in healthy, confortable ways.

___ 22. with my ability to relate in ways in which people can see my humanity.

___ 23. with my ability to relate to others in sexually appropriate ways.

___ 24. with my ability to show people my appreciation for them in a clear manner.

___ 25. with the degree to which I can ask people for psychological, spiritual, and pastoral help when I need it.

Part III: Ministerial Life

___ 1. with the degree to which people can see Jesus in me.

___ 2. with the degree to which ministry is my full-time vocation and not just a profession that is practiced forty hours a week.

___ 3. with my ability to accept my failures in a growth-producing way.

___ 4. with my ability to keep confidential all information that would reflect negatively on another person.

___ 5. with my ability to do good without letting others know about it.

___ 6. with my ability to treat nonministers as equals.

___ 7. with the degree to which I delegate authority and share power.

___ 8. with the degree to which I allow parishioners the freedom to do what they feel is best.

___ 9. with my ability to be open to and try new ideas.

___ 10. with the degree to which I keep the parishioners abreast of the newest issues in theology and spirituality.

___ 11. with the care with which I prepare my presentations.

___ 12. with the degree to which I keep current with the ministerial literature and attend classes and workshops.

___ 13. with the manner in which I respect and study related fields, such as psychology, sociology, group dynamics.

___ 14. with my ability to admit my own confusion, conflict, questioning, and doubt with regard to religion or the Church.

___ 15. with my ability to strike a good balance between loyalty to the people, to myself, and to reality.

___ 16. with my ability to relate well with people whose behavior or life-style is different or contrary to the Church's teaching.

___ 17. with the degree to which I educate people to form their own consciences.

___ 18. with the degree to which I work to bring about the changes necessary in ministry.

___ 19. with the degree to which I refer people to other ministers or professionals when it is appropriate.

___ 20. with my willingness to actively recruit parish leaders.

___ 21. with my ability to see the law as a means to an end and not an end in itself.

___ 22. with my ability to see and admit to errors and imperfections in the Church.

___ 23. with the degree to which I am familiar with the valid insights of other denominations and relate to members and ministers of other denominations.

___ 24. with the degree to which I decline to participate in professional activities for which I am not fully qualified.

___ 25. with my ability to recognize the difference between spiritual direction and amateur counseling.

Part IV: Spiritual Life

___ 1. with the amount of time I spend in meditation, contemplation, and prayer each day.

___ 2. with the quality, depth, and meaningfulness of my prayer.

___ 3. with the amount of overall growth I can attribute to my prayer life.

___ 4. with the intimacy, comfort, security, and joy I find in my relationship with God.

___ 5. with the amount and kinds of spiritual reading I do.

___ 6. with the degree to which I pray and discuss spiritual issues with other ministers.

___ 7. with the degree that I integrate my prayer into the rest of the day.

___ 8. with the number of times I meet with a spiritual director.

___ 9. with my real knowledge and appreciation of Scripture (both the Old and New Testaments).

___ 10. with how far my spiritual life has progressed over the past year.

___ 11. with my ability to live the gospel values of poverty, love, justice, tolerance, compassion, freedom, and forgiveness.

___ 12. with the degree that my liturgical and sacramental life is deeply and personally meaningful to me.

___ 13. with the degree to which my fear of dying and death has diminished as a result of deepening faith.

___ 14. with the degree I am increasing my knowledge of God the Father and the Holy Spirit.

___ 15. with the degree that I am able to admit to some religious questions and doubts.

___ 16. with the degree that I have specific subgoals and goals toward which I am striving in my spiritual life.

___ 17. with my ability to see meaning in my periods of spiritual aridity and desolation.

___ 18. with my ability to listen to God's voice in my prayer and in my daily experience.

___ 19. with the degree to which I am familiar with the lives of the saints and learn something of value from them with regard to my own life.

___ 20. with the degree to which I am open, accepting, and freeing of myself and others.

___ 21. with the degree I can see God as an unconditionally loving parent or benevolent friend.

___ 22. with the degree to which my spiritual life leads and motivates me to become involved with social justice issues, the poor in spirit (which includes both the materially poor and the materially wealthy), the sick, the elderly, the imprisoned, and those disenfranchised by the Church and society.

___ 23. with the degree to which I learn about other types of spirituality (Catholic, Protestant, Eastern, Mystical, Charismatic).

___ 24. with the degree to which my spirituality helps me place the glorious and traumatic events of the world in a proper perspective.

___ 25. with the degree that my spirituality is an inspiration and not a burden or distraction to others.

Using the Evaluation

When you are finished with the entire self-evaluation form, place one check (√) next to each item marked with a B; place two checks next to each item you marked with a C; and place three checks next to each item you marked with a D. This will help you identify areas that you may wish to work on.

There are several ways that you can use the results of this evaluation. One way is to write down on a separate page one item with one check mark, another item with two check marks, and a third item with three check marks. These three items can be used as growth goals for a period of two weeks or a month until you feel you have brought each item up at least one, if not two or three, points. This process can then be repeated with three more items. Using this approach helps to concretize growth goals so that they constitute a clear and measurable target. Moreover, the specific items can be used as material in meditation, prayer, personal counseling, and spiritual direction. It can also be interesting and helpful to fill out a fresh form every year to see where growth, fixation, or regression has occurred.

In situations in which you are supervising a person—in pastoral care work, for example—this evaluation can be used as an instrument for discussion, learning, and evaluation. You can have the person fill out the self-evaluation and then discuss it together; or you can each fill out the evaluation, except you can fill out some of the sections in the light in which you see the person. Points of agreement or discrepancies can then be focal points for discussion and learning.

If the members of a ministerial team trust each other enough, the forms can be filled out by each minister and then shared with the others. Then each minister, and the team as a group, can help each member work on areas of dissatisfaction.

Parish Evaluative Questionnaire

Directions: We are interested in what you think is good about our parish and what you think needs improvement. Please take ten minutes of your time to fill out this questionnaire. In the space in front of each statement, write the letter that best reflects your reaction to the statement:

A. This statement is *true most of the time.*
B. This statement is *more true than false.*
C. This statement is *more false than true.*
D. This statement is *false most of the time.*
E. I have no way of knowing whether or not this statement is true.

For example:
____ The sermons in our parish are well presented and helpful.

If you believe this statement to be more true than false, but not true most of the time, place a B in the blank. Please try to fill out the entire questionnaire, leaving none of the spaces blank. Thank you.

___ 1. The ordained minister(s) is(are) available and willing to help when called upon.

___ 2. I would feel comfortable going to the ordained minister(s) for personal help.

___ 3. The ordained ministers live life-styles and behave in ways that are in keeping with the values they should symbolize.

___ 4. The sermons are well prepared and well delivered, and are helpful.

___ 5. The services and liturgies are well-done and a source of inspiration.

___ 6. The parish offers a sufficient number of religious services and spiritual presentations and events.

___ 7. The parish has a friendly and helpful spirit.

___ 8. The leadership in the parish is effective and helpful.

___ 9. The religious education programs effectively meet the needs of the children (ages to 14).

___ 10. The religious education programs effectively meet the needs of the high school students.

___ 11. The parish has an effective adult religious education program.

___ 12. The parish effectively meets the spiritual needs of the infirm, elderly, and handicapped.

___ 13. The parish meets the needs of upper and lower income people equally well.

___ 14. The parish has effective programs for special groups (single adults, divorced and separated people, minorities, etc.).

___ 15. The parish actively solicits help from the people.

___ 16. Nonordained ministers and other lay people play an important role in the parish.

___ 17. The parish uses lay ministers (i.e., nonordained ministers who teach religion, visit the sick, help the poor, participate in religious services, etc.) in ways that strengthen the parish.

___ 18. The relationship between the ordained ministers and the lay ministers seems to be healthy and effective.

___ 19. The parish actively solicits people to share their gifts by becoming lay ministers in our parish.

___ 20. The parish keeps the people informed with respect to its needs, programs, activities.

___ 21. The parish handles its finances in an open and sensible way.

___ 22. The parish is concerned with social justice issues beyond the parish boundaries.

___ 23. The parish has a sufficient number of educational functions (speakers, panels, workshops).

Please fill in the blanks after each of the following statements with your most honest reaction.

1. The thing I like best about our parish is _____
   _____ .

2. The thing I like least about our parish is   _____
   _____ .

3. I think the parish leadership _____ .

4. If I were the pastor, I would   _____ .

5. The reason most people don't actively participate (that is, do more than attend services and donate money) in the parish is that _____
   _____ .

6. As far as personally taking an active role in the parish, I _____
   _____ .

7. If someone asked me to describe our parish in five words or less, I would say, "Our parish is . . .
   _____ _____   _____ _____   _____ ."

Please feel free to add any of your own comments and to sign your name to this questionnaire or to remain anonymous, as you wish. Thank you very much for taking your time to fill out this questionnaire, and please feel free to give us feedback at any time.

_____

_____

_____

*   *   *   *

This parish questionnaire is just a sample of the types of evaluations that ministers can devise. It is purposely general in nature.

Ministers can add items that are particularly tailored to their own situations.

An important item to include in any questionnaire of this nature is, "I have no way of knowing whether or not this statement is true." When this answer is given, it raises the question, "Why doesn't this person know about this area of parish life?" It could be that the area is simply not one with which the person is familiar, but it could just as easily reflect a poor communication system in the parish.

In summary, both ministerial self-evaluations and parish evaluations are criticially important if ministers and parishes are going to remain effective and alive. Evaluation results are like navigational signals that reflect whether ministers and parishes are on course, straying from their courses, or dead in the water. Whatever the case, it is important information to have. Statements such as "No evaluation form is adequate to give us a reliable reading," "What do the *people* know about what constitutes a good parish?" and "We'll just get answers of all kinds, and they'll just cancel each other out," sound more like rationalizations of insecure people than astute and honest observations.

MEDITATIONS FOR MINISTERS

Like formal prayer and contemplation, meditation is an important part of one's spiritual life. The following are some meditations of a psycho-spiritual nature which are specifically tailored to ministers. Obviously, Scripture embodies an endless source of material for meditation. The meditations offered here are from the thoughts of contemporary ministers and can serve as an adjunct to Scripture. Ministers may use these meditations and the questions which follow each one in ways with which they feel most comfortable. Some ministers may wish to meditate silently; others may wish to jot down their meditations to concretize them or use them for future reference. In discussion groups, ministers may share their meditations and respond to one another's meditations.

It is possible that this or that particular quote will not spark any worthwhile response. When this occurs, it may be simply that the meditation does not touch the minister in any meaningful way. However, it may also mean that the thought is subconsciously threatening, and the minister wants to avoid it. Therefore, before a thought is prematurely discarded, it should be given a second consideration.

Several of the meditative thoughts are quotations that assume that all ministers are male by using words such as "clergyman," and "he" or "him" to refer to ministers. However, in keeping with the theme of this book, the term "minister" refers to females as well as males and to nonordained as well as ordained people.

I. The realization that one is on a pilgrimage is of greater value than having all the answers. In this context clergy and laity are fellow pilgrims. When the clergy are free of the "answer man" role, they are more able to hear. (James C. Fenhagen, *Mutual Ministry*)[1]

- Do I view myself as a fellow traveler, as one among many who needs to explore new frontiers, or have I appointed myself, or allowed myself to be appointed, the veteran explorer who knows the way?
- What have I heard from the people I serve this week that has increased my understanding of myself, people, or God?
- Am I able to invite others to share their thoughts and feelings with me so that I can become a better minister, or do I, at least implicitly, communicate the message, "You have nothing of substance to teach me about myself, you, Christianity, faith, or God"?

II. The [minister] who permits himself to grow discouraged because the vast majority of his parishioners will not respond to him even when his conviction is the strongest and his preaching of the Word most articulate and his compassion most sensitive, displays a very naive assumption about the nature of human nature and little understanding of the saving remnant of the Old Testament or of the "failure" of the mission of Jesus in the New. (Andrew M. Greeley, "Priest, Church, and the Future from a Sociological Viewpoint," in *Future Forms of Ministry*)[2]

- What are my reactions when I "give it my best shot," and I fall short of the mark? Do I say to Jesus, "Now I know a little about how you felt," or do I blame myself and/or other people?
- When I think I've begun a good pastoral relationship with a person or couple, and they "disappear" after one or a few meetings, how do I feel? Do I feel like giving up my pastoral efforts? Do I hunt the people down and chastise them (albeit in a "Christian" way)? Do I realize that Christ himself may not have been able to do any better?
- Do I realize that, in doing the best I can in a situation, I may have planted a seed that, over a period of time, may bear fruit, or do I expect all seeds to bear immediate fruit?

III. It is more difficult in some ways for a [minister] to preserve his spiritual life than it is for a layman. Because religion is his vocation it can easily become professionalized. He is so identified with it that its professionalization may extend even into his solitude. Where then is the religious person behind the religious professional? I would imagine that a comparable situation could occur with a professional ball player. Playing ball is for enjoyment. But what happens to this enjoyment when playing ball becomes one's work? Is it then any longer play? (William E. Hulme, *Your Pastor's Problems*)[3]

- Is my spiritual life (prayer, solitude, and spiritual reading) alive and enjoyable, or has it become mostly "duty time" or a luxury? Or, has it become extinct?
- Do I reserve adequate and private time each day for my spiritual life, or do I rationalize that my good works adequately take the place of a spiritual life?

- Do I pray in private, or do I consider my rote, sometimes distracted public prayers all the prayer I need or have time for?

IV. The gospel is trivialized by irrelevance. Reinhold Niebuhr was pointing to this sort of possibility when he said that the worst evils in the world are not done by evil men; the worst evils in the world are done by good men who do not know that they are not doing good. (Fred Brown, *Faith without Religion*)[4]

- When I say to myself, "I think I'll do such and such because it would be good for me," do I give as much consideration to the possibility it could be bad for me?
- When I say to myself, "I don't think I'll do such and such because it will be bad for me," do I give as much consideration to the possibility it could be good for me?
- When I am harsh with people, is it for their own good, or could it be that it makes me feel good?
- What I am supportive of people, is it for their own good, or could it be that it makes me feel good?
- Do I seek feedback from an objective colleague when I'm not sure whether I am about to do good or harm, or do I trust all my inclinations without reservation?

V. At a clergy conference typical of a number of such gatherings, I recall making the point that the spiritual life is necessarily subversive of our fondest assumptions about ourselves.... (Urban T. Holmes, III, *Spirituality for Ministers*)[5]

- What are some of my fondest assumptions about myself?
- How large is the distance between these assumptions and reality?
- In my spiritual life, have I learned anything about myself that has reduced or nullified any of my fondest assumptions?
- Do I fight to hold on to my fondest assumptions about myself, even when my spiritual life teaches me they are untrue?

VI. People like myself have a love-hate relationship with the Church. She infuriates us, yet we cannot do without her. We would often like to leave her, but where else would we go? (Ernest Marvin, "Ministry in Ferment," in *Ministry in Question*)[6]

- Do I have ambivalent feelings toward the Church, or do I love its good points and ignore its bad points, like a star-struck teenager?
- If I have ambivalent feelings toward the Church, how do I handle them? Do I use them in constructive ways to strengthen the weaknesses in me and/or in the Church, or do I use them as an excuse to live on the periphery of ministry and/or Christianity?
- Do I allow others to have a love-hate relationship with the Church, or do I directly or subtly chastise them, even when their ambivalence is well-founded?

VII. A minister who cannot tolerate ambiguity cannot tolerate a local church. In many respects, as we now know, the capacity to tolerate ambiguity is a kind of final mark of mental health. One may be low on it [tolerance] and still mentally healthy if the external situation can be arranged to make it [the tolerance of ambiguity] unnecessary. But for all complex services and positions, this capacity may make the difference between success and failure. If a minister has very little such capacity, then that is the situation; and the Lord will obviously want him working elsewhere than in a local church. (Seward Hiltner, *Ferment in the Ministry*)[7]

- How well do I tolerate confusion, lack of clarity, and things being up in the air? Do I react with patience and use the ambiguity for growth, or do I rush in and prematurely push for a solution in order to decrease my anxiety?
- When it looks as if a situation is clear, how do I react if someone raises an issue that confuses the situation? Do I view him

or her as throwing a monkey wrench into the works, or as a person who sees a dimension which I did not see but which deserves consideration?

- How do I handle not knowing how important situations will turn out? Do I wait patiently until the situation gets resolved, or do I fret and worry about it?

VIII. As a human person, the [minister] desires to live on forever. He needs to be recognized, and appreciates the warmth of being loved. Like any other human being, the [minister] wants to be accepted. He wants to belong, to be and to feel needed. He, like other men, passes through various discernible stages in life's growth. He has the need for some recognition of his efforts and respect for his person. Like others, he searches for intimacy with his God, and struggles to integrate his life in the presence of the Lord. It is important to recognize these ordinary needs. They help in understanding much of the frustration, tension, and conflict experienced by priests. If the priest does not understand that they are calling for fulfillment within him, his attitudes will be troubled and poorly developed. He will experience anxieties which he does not comprehend. He may well confuse some of his natural yearnings with moral shortcomings. (U.S. Catholic Conference, *As One Who Serves*)[8]

- What are my two greatest human needs, and how well am I getting them met?
- Since I alone am responsible for their fulfillment, what could *I* do to meet my needs better?
- What excuses do I give myself and others for not getting my needs met?
- Do I downplay my needs as too human, secular, weak, dangerous, and, if so, why?
- How well do I allow and help other ministers to meet their human needs for security, acceptance, freedom, and appreciation?

IX. Man has come of age in religion. He can no longer shift his own responsibility on to the voice of the past. He may be anxious about his task, but he can no longer avoid it. (Gerd Theissen, *A Critical Faith*)⁹

- How do I make Scripture relevant in today's world?
- Is my personal life and ministry built on the foundations of "The Bible says," "The Church says," "Tradition teaches"? And is what was relevant five hundred or two thousand years ago always directly relevant to today's world?
- Do I try to appeal to these legitimate sources of knowledge, but also to sift them through my own experience and the experience of Christians in the twentieth century? In other words, do I merely mouth Church history, or do I *make* Church history by participating daily in the religious renovation that is necessary to keep Christianity strong and credible?

X. The often unconscious conspiracy between lay persons and [the minister] produces a bargain in which both parties agree to certain conditions in return for certain rewards—just like marriage. One person [the minister] is allowed to feel in charge at the expense of feeling a little set apart and insecure. The other person [the lay person] is allowed to feel cared for and secure at the expense of feeling slightly inferior and with less power. (James C. Fenhagen, *Mutual Ministry*)¹⁰

- As is true with any relationship, am I aware that the relationship between myself and the people I serve is full of unconscious negotiations?
- What types of unconscious negotiations are present between myself and the people I serve? Do I understand that the cause of most relationship problems is that one party has violated the unconscious "deal" that has been agreed upon?
- Am I able to give up being in charge for the feeling of a healthy belonging with the people I serve?

XI. Some . . . ministers . . . are often inclined to believe that the good they do makes them more worthy in the sight of God. The preaching, counseling, and caring that I do give proof (I hope) of my own goodness, even perhaps earning my salvation. Few of us would consciously hold this theological position, but this deep-seated hope may lie at the root of some of our compulsiveness and busy-ness in ministry. Again, if we participate in this kind of compulsiveness, it may be revealed in a reflection on our use of time. If we are compelled to "earn our way" with God, to repeatedly prove our worth by what we achieve in the vineyard of the Lord, then nonachievement time will appear a waste and be avoided. Time for prayer will lose its value because I am not *doing* anything, not helping anyone. Leisure time and vacation, which share the "uselessness" of time for prayer, will be avoided or at least apologized for. (James D. Whitehead and Evelyn Eaton Whitehead, *Method in Ministry*)[11]

- Do I believe and feel that God loves me for who I am and not for what I do?
- Is the ministerial axiom "all things to all people" an ideal for me, or is it a prerequisite for being loved by God and for defining myself as a minister?
- I tell others that God unconditionally loves them, but do I really believe that God unconditionally loves *me*?
- Must I work myself into illness and an early death to justify my existence?
- Do I view life as a celebration as much as I view it as a tough assignment with a short deadline?

XII. Likely candidates for clerical burnout are the romantics, who believe that they possess a boundless source of love and care. What feeds this illusion is the feeling that they [the clergy] have to be a perfect reflection of the "image of God." . . . I am convinced that this is no exaggeration; many priests and pastors work themselves into an impossible situation based precisely on this belief. Such attempted omnipotence, coupled with a sentimental motivation, is doomed to quick exhaustion. (Urban T. Holmes, III, *Spirituality for Mutual Ministry*)[12]

- Do I work at a pace that allows me to be optimally effective a great deal of the time, or do I stretch myself so thin that too many people do not relate with me but only to scraps of me?
- Do I define my worth and justify my existence by my work, or by how well I live out the gospel virtues of kindness, honesty, justice, freedom, forgiveness, and faith?
- Do I have a realisitc appraisal of my limitations, or do I harbor some romantic rescue fantasies that lead me to overextend myself to the detriment of myself and others?
- What would happen to me psychologically and spiritually if, for whatever reason, I was forced to work only twenty hours each week?

XIII. [Cardinal John Henry Newman] not only had learning, style, and precision, but also the experience of a long and lonely search for truth. Part of his influence is due to his unusual training, for he was, in turn, Evangelical, Calvinist, Church of England, founder of the High Church movement, and finally, Roman Catholic. (Bernard Bassett, *And Would You Believe It!*)[13]

- What does this statement mean to me? If I'm Roman Catholic, does it mean that Newman, after years of searching, finally found the truth in Roman Catholicism?
- If I'm an Anglican, does it mean that Newman, as intelligent as he was, lacked the ability to understand reformation theology properly?
- Whatever denomination I am, do I see that there are many paths to the Kingdom, and that there are important things to be learned from all Christian denominations as well as all other religions?

- Can I believe that if Newman had also been Jewish, he would have been an even greater thinker? Or, do I need to feel secure that my religion is all I really need to become the fullest person I can?

XIV. But if we are bogged down and are not growing, then the sensible, intelligent, mature thing to do is seek help where it can be found. It is a terribly hard thing for any presumed adult male to admit he cannot solve his problems by himself. It can be especially difficult for a priest to admit this. (Andrew M. Greeley, *Uncertain Trumpet*)[14]

- When I experience difficulties that interfere with my levels of energy, effectiveness, and happiness, do I feel free to contact a spiritual director or a counselor, or do I so strongly define myself as a helper and not as a helpee that I cannot seek help for myself?
- How would I view myself if I sought counseling? As a normal and good person who needs some help? Or as an abnormal, weak person who cannot solve his or her own problems?
- If I view myself as less of a person should I need help, how does this view affect my view of the people who seek help from me?

XV. It is not the task of the Christian leader to go around nervously trying to redeem people, to save them at the last minute, to put them on the right track. For we are called to help others affirm this great news, and to make visible in daily events the fact that behind the dirty curtain of our painful symptoms there is something great to be seen: the face of Him in whose image we are shaped. (Henri J. M. Nouwen, *The Wounded Healer*)[15]

- Do I nervously go around trying to prevent problems for people or rescue them from their problems, as if that is the main purpose for which I was placed on earth?
- Do I understand that, while it is legitimate to help people solve their problems, I can become so problem-centered and allow

others to remain so problem-centered as to squeeze Jesus out of the picture?

- Do I spend more time asking myself, "How will I solve this problem?" rather than asking, "What will I learn from this problem regarding myself, others, and God?"
- Do I *really* believe that we *are* redeemed, or do I act mostly as if we are not, and spend my time as a spiritual ambulance chaser?

XVI. Christians have sometimes focused on an afterlife to the point where "getting into heaven" is the only real motive for religious practice. It is no secret that many Christians have gone to church weekly not mainly to give praise and thanks to God, but as a security measure, a duty that will guarantee a heavenly reward. The preoccupation with getting to heaven is a considerable change in focus from the message of the prophets and of Jesus, who were always preoccupied with our relationship with God in *this* world. If Christians have at times slipped into a heaven-oriented religion, we should also be aware that this tendency is a very ancient one. (Tad Guzie, *The Book of Sacramental Basics*)[16]

- Deep down, how much of my personal and interpersonal ministry is connected with getting into heaven?
- What changes would occur in my life and my relationships with people if God came to earth and announced that there is no afterlife, that we shall disappear into a nonbeing at death?
- How much do I truly care about myself and others, and how much are my life and ministry parts of an eternal life insurance policy?
- How much do I, at least unconsciously, view others as spiritual stepping-stones to heaven?

XVII. After all, it is a dogma of the Church that no man or woman without some special grace can long avoid serious sin. It's the way we're made. But if every serious sin is mortal, deadly, completely destructive of the relationship with God, we might as well all give up. (William J. O'Malley, *The Roots of Unbelief*)[17]

- What are the two most serious sins that I've committed?
- Why were they "serious"? Because someone said they were, or because I did serious damage to myself, another, or my relationship with God?
- What "demon" overcame me and caused me to commit the sin: greed, lust, anger, or selfishness?
- How have I been different since I've committed those serious sins? Have I accepted my sinfulness, learned from it, and done better when similar situations arose, or did I give up a little on myself, others, God, or life without even realizing it?
- Do I truly understand that God *expects* us to sin and is mostly interested in what we do with our guilt and shame—whether we use it to grow in wisdom, strength, and compassion, or whether we use it as an excuse to give up?

XVIII. A Christian [minister] should expect failure so that it may not destroy his hope in the gospel. Failure is a result of the brokenness of this world and is the inevitable product of risk. The [minister] who never fails is the [minister] who never allows God to create a new wholeness through him. Whereas I would not go so far as to seek failure and despise success, it is true to say that the [minister] is called to be faithful, not successful. (Urban T. Holmes, III, *The Priest in Community*)[18]

- Do I *allow* myself to fail, or do I typically avoid situations in which I could experience a sense of failure?
- Do I tend to personalize failure (*I* failed), or do I understand that it is possible to do everything reasonably well and still fail because of factors I cannot control? Or, do I typically absolve myself of all personal failure by blaming other people and situations?

- How do I normally react to failure? Do I learn from it and try again, or do I decide never to try that particular task again?
- How do I relate to other ministers who fail? Do I empathize and help, or do I criticize and avoid them?

XIX. Sincere prayer opens us to the needs of others and prepares us to do what is in our power to assist our brothers in need. Genuine prayer for peace and unity transforms us into instruments of peace and unity. (Bernard Haring, *Faith and Morality in the Secular Age*)[19]

- Am I the kind of minister who continually prays for peace, justice, love, compassion, and reconciliation in the world, yet does absolutely nothing to bring them about? Or, are my prayers both the cause and effect of my daily behavior that pursues these virtues?
- Are my public prayers simply pep talks, meant to exhort people to infuse Christian values into their lives while I remain on the sidelines, or is my entire day and week a prayer?
- What specific thing have I done this week to further the cause of justice, compassion, and freedom?

XX. Religion is always given a bad name, and faith seems like a soggy burden when it is urged by people who do not believe fundamentally in the capacity of other people at all. These people shield themselves from others and thus make themselves unbelievable. Nothing is emptier than sermons on faith in God preached by clergy who cannot believe in persons. Unbelieving ritual gestures made in the name of such faith are probably the most obscene gesture in the history of the world. (Eugene C. Kennedy, *Believing*)[20]

- How much do I believe in *myself*, in my capacity to be more loving, patient, tolerant, holy, unselfish, disciplined, free, strong, peaceful, effective?
- Is there a part of me I do not trust or have given up on?

- What *specifically* don't I trust in other people?
- Do I understand the difference between acceptance of self and others as an end in itself and acceptance for the purpose of attempting change?
- What is one behavior in myself that I do not particularly like, but which I pretend that I cannot do anything about?

XXI. Having grown up as a pleaser, a placater, a knee-jerk nice guy, I entered the ministry full of messiah needs. "They have to appreciate me," I thought, "especially since I've been so helpful to them." But they didn't. Once their pain has subsided, or their dependency is outgrown or outmaneuvered, people don't any longer care much for the nice-guy savior and helper. (David W. Augsburger, *Anger and Assertiveness in Pastoral Care*)[21]

- How much of the time am I a "nice person" in contrast to a "real person"?
- Is there a relationship between my being a "nice person" and people not taking me very seriously?
- Does my "nice person" façade hide resentments? What are they?
- What would happen to me and others if I just was *me* for seven days in a row?
- Since it is clear that Jesus was not always "nice," why do I think being nicer than Jesus is good or Christian?
- When I am not *myself* with people, am I showing disrespect for them? For myself?

XXII. Human freedom is only secondarily freedom *from* limitations and threats. Primarily it is freedom *for*. (Karl Barth, "The Gift of Freedom: Foundation of Evangelical Ethics")[22]

- What has the freedom that comes from my human nature and ministry freed me *for*?
- Am I free enough to take an unpopular stand?
- Am I free enough to make the decisions in my life that signifi-

cantly affect my welfare, or do I suppress my freedom in the interests of the wishes of others?

• Does my freedom *from* secular constraints free me *for* a warmer and closer relationship with people?

XXIII. No wonder Jesus' family thought he was out of his mind. The scribes' diagnosis might have been a kinder one, only that he was possessed by Beelzebub. (James E. Dittes, *Minister on the Spot*)[23]

• If his own family and religious teachers thought that Jesus was "off base," do I truly understand how readily this can happen to me if I function as a true minister and prophet?

• If my deep beliefs and values are different from my famliy's and superiors', how do I handle it? Do I pretend that they are not different? Do I use my beliefs and values as weapons, or do I own them and communicate them in constructive ways?

XXIV. Ministers must be able to shake off disappointments, hurt feelings, insults, flattery, coaxing, and then go about their business. In other words, they must be grown-ups and completely *self-controlled*. (Hartzell Spence, *The Clergy and What They Do*)[24]

• How well do I shake off hurt feelings, flattery, and coaxing? Am I able to shake off all three, or do I shake off hurt feelings, but cling to flattery? Or, do I shake off flattery, but cling to hurt feelings? Do I shake off coaxing, or does it depend upon who's doing the coaxing?

• How self-controlled am I? Do I follow my own lights when I have good reason to believe they are true, or do I allow the winds of criticism, rejection, manipulation, and flattery to blow me off course?

XXV. We have fallen into the temptation of separating ministry from spirituality, service from prayer. Our demon says: "We are too busy to pray; we have too many needs to attend to, too many people to respond to, too many wounds to heal. Prayer is a luxury, something to do during a free hour, a day away from work or on a retreat. (Henri J. M. Nouwen, *The Living Reminder*)[25]

- Is my spiritual life an integral part of my life, opening each morning and putting closure on each day, or is it so "spiritual" that no one can see it, including myself and God?
- Do I truly understand that being too busy for a spiritual life raises the same questions and concerns as a situation in which a man is too busy to communicate with his wife? In other words, what are the *real* issues I don't want to communicate with God?
- Do I work on the axiom that my apostolic work is my prayer and is an adequate substitute for a more direct spiritual and prayer life with God? If I do, what would I tell a husband who says that his work is the best way he can communicate his love for his wife and children?

XXVI. It is not only that religion runs the perpetual risk of hypocrisy, but that religion is not the substance of salvation. When Jesus himself talks about how man will fare beyond death, it is noteworthy that religion in no way comes into the discussion. In the parable of judgment, in Matthew 25, Jesus infers that men will be judged neither by their religious fidelity nor by the specific religious commandments of Israel. They will be judged on whether or not they have fed, housed, clothed, refreshed, healed, or consoled their neighbor in need. . . . He is constantly drawing attention away from ritual activities, from religion, from what is specifically intra-church, to the secular, material service of neighbor in need. Thus the purpose of religion is to lead men to salvation, but not to replace these salvific acts with others of its own making. (James Tunstead Burtchaell, *Philemon's Problem: The Daily Dilemma of the Christian*)[26]

- Do I really understand the differences between Christianity and religion, and do I see specific points of conflict between the two?
- How much of my personal life is occupied by my being a religionist? How much by my being a Christian?
- As a minister, how much of my work reflects my private, subconscious religious biases and how much reflects the teachings of Jesus Christ?

XXVII. The Bible says very little about what a clergyman should do. It says a great deal, however, about what kind of a person he should be. (Hartzell Spence, *The Clergy and What They Do*)[27]

- Do I tend to define my identity by who I am with people or what I do for people?
- Would I prefer to be judged by God according to who I am or what I do?
- Do I realize that who I am eventually shows through my words and actions, or do I think that my words and actions can hide what I'm actually thinking or feeling?
- Who do I think I *should* be as a minister? On a scale of one to ten, where do I fall in this regard?

XXVIII. We can see the [minister] as believer only when we see him [or her] as unbeliever. Every belief we establish for ourselves puts us in the position of disbelieving in something else. Our system of disbelief is as important to us as our system of belief. This is all the more so since they often coexist in us; we are like the man in the gospels who pleaded with Jesus: "I believe, Lord, help my unbelief." (David P. O'Neill, *The Priest in Crisis*)[28]

- As a Christian minister, do I believe everything that I am "supposed" to believe, or can I admit that I have questions and doubts?
- If I believe all Christian dogmas, doctrines, and teachings, does this belief flow from a faith fashioned from study, prayer, life

experiences, and grace, or is it more of a blind faith founded on a good deal of suppression of doubt and romantic and hopeful thinking?

- If I do have some questions and doubts, what specific teachings are problematic for me, and what can I learn about myself, the Church, and God through my uncertainty?

XXIX. The virtue of prudence has often been falsified in the Church in a very time-serving way: made to mean being careful only to say what is opportune; i.e., what is pleasing to those in charge. This meant overlooking the fact that in the New Testament caution plays only a small role, frankness a large one. The Greek word *parresia* is so often used there, in the sense of the openness that does not hush up or conceal anything, of the frankness that feels no embarrassment, of the boldness that has no fear. (Hans Kung, *Freedom Today*)[29]

- Do I have a proper understanding of the virtue of prudence?
- What does prudence mean to me? Constructively communicating honest thoughts, feelings, and reactions? Or stating only those things that will not upset people?
- If God guaranteed that, regardless of what I taught, preached, or counseled, I would be fully loved by my family, friends, parishioners, and superiors, would there be any specific areas about which I would be more honest, frank, or bold?
- If Jesus were alive today, what might he say to the Church, to the clergy, and to the people at large that I would be delighted to hear because I lack the courage to say it?

XXX. Unfortunately, it is not an exaggeration to say that many [ministers] do not read much, and that some [ministers] do not read at all. The anti-intellectualism and the lack of education among clergy might have been tolerable three decades ago when our population had less education than it does now, but it is certainly not tolerable now. If so many sermons sound like the [minister] has nothing to say, the reason is that he does indeed have nothing to say and he has nothing to say because he hasn't thought seriously about anything for a long time, and is still leaning back on his seminary notes for his religious ideas. (Andrew Greeley, Mark Durkin, John Shea, David Tracy, and William McCready, *Parish, Priest, and People*)[30]

- How many hours each week do I invest in becoming a more effective and competent teacher, preacher, counselor, spiritual director, and celebrant?
- Do I keep up with my vocation and profession the way a good physician, attorney, or professor does; or do I believe that my personality, sense of humor, and hard work compensate for my lapsing professional competencies?
- Do I regularly update and refine my skills, or do I think that my daily pastoral preparations and experiences are adequate substitutes for reading, courses, and workshops?

XXXI. It seems clear that, in the present situation, the [minister] can no longer be satisfied with being in the Christian community merely a "cult priest," a dispenser of the sacraments and the celebrant of the Eucharist, as he is still far too often even today. . . . Such a purely cultural role would make the [minister] into a living anachronism and give the impression of his being the dispenser of some kind of "medieval magic." In our time far more than in the past, the [minister] has to be, not only the man who, through his ritual action, provides the channel for Christ's sacramental grace, but also the man who, through the animation and the education of the faith of the receivers, makes Christ's salvific presence in the sacraments really effective. (Joseph J. Blomjous, *Priesthood in Crisis*)[31]

- Do I truly understand the critical differences between being a "cult priest" and a pastoral minister, or, if I am to be absolutely honest with myself, am I mostly a "dispenser of sacraments"?

- Do I animate the people? Do I bring them alive by sharing the good news?
- Do I educate the people, that is, draw out and actualize their religious needs and values, or do I share religious facts with them that often are not "facts" at all?

XXXII. We need only look at many of the [ministers] we know to realize that, in spite of all their work and generosity, they are frightened of really loving their people and permitting them to love them in return. Worship and admiration from a distance is fine, but human love up close is terrifying. So [ministers] grow old hiding behind their [clerical] collars, crouching in fear behind the altar, defining inhumanity as piety, and refusing to let that which is most noble in them emerge. (Andrew M. Greeley, *Uncertain Trumpet*)[32]

- How well do I allow myself to get emotionally close to people, and how well do I protect myself from human closeness, using my vocation (of love) as an excuse?
- When I see people expressing deep affection toward each other, can I psychologically share in that experience, or does it strike a note of pain in me because of an unfulfilled need in my own life?
- Do I believe that each day is a new invitation to begin a love relationship, or do I believe that it's too late to begin loving people on a deep, personal level?

XXXIII. As a man among men [Jesus] appeared externally to those around him in exactly the same way as any other human individual appears. He experienced fatigue, hunger, disappointment, loneliness, and the usual limitations in knowledge that belong to the human condition. (Dermot A. Lane, *The Reality of Jesus*)[33]

- What does striving to become Christ-like mean to me? Besides being loving, forgiving, generous and compassionate, do I realize that becoming Christ-like also means being tired (of addressing the same situations day after day), hungry (for love, attention, affirmation), disappointed (because what I had hoped would come true for myself and others has not), lonely (feeling alone and abandoned in spite of all the people who love me), and feeling frustratingly ignorant (because I sometimes do not see problems until after I've created them)?

- How do I react to people who come to me feeling the burden of the human qualities described above? Is my first articulated or non-articulated reaction, "Oh, dear, you shouldn't feel that way."?

- Do I use my fatigue, hunger, disappointment, loneliness, and ignorance as excuses to regress or as opportunities to grow?

CONCLUSION

In summary, this chapter has tried to present a mirror in which ministers can see and evaluate themselves. Of course, ministers can relate to a mirror in a variety of ways; and the way they choose to relate will make a difference in their own and their ministry's health and exercise.

If they so choose, ministers can look only at their attractive parts, pretending that their ordinary and unattractive aspects do not exist. Unfortunately, this too often causes them to overplay their hand and results in their participating in "sins of commission." In other words, ministers who refuse to see their unattractive sides often end up saying and doing injudicious and damaging things to themselves and to others.

Ministers can look into the mirror and see only their ordinary and unattractive parts, pretending that their attractive qualities do not exist. This usually causes ministers to underplay their hand and results in their committing "sins of omission." In other words, ministers who refuse to see their attractive sides too often fail to reach out to people in ways that would be beneficial both to others and to themselves.

Ministers can walk right past the mirror without ever looking into it. These ministers believe that their positive and negative self-delusions represent reality. The effects on themselves and on their ministry will be similar to those mentioned above.

Finally, ministers can look into the mirror and allow themselves a full, unexpurgated view. This clear view allows them to assess accurately what is good, average, and imperfect about themselves and their ministry and to make appropriate and desirable changes.

Clearly, the best indication of a minister's psychological health is the ability to look at oneself objectively *and* to make the appropriate changes. Most people cannot look at themselves objectively because the view is too threatening. Some people can look at themselves objectively but are unwilling to make any real changes. Others are forever making changes but not ones based on a true reflection of themselves. If ministers can learn and can teach others how to be more personally reflective—that is, how to elicit and accept clear, personal, evaluative information—ministers and those they serve will discover that change and growth will be an exciting process in their ministry and lives.

Epilogue

Of all the vocations a Christian can have in this world, the ministerial life is, at different times, the most uplifting and the most discouraging; the most exciting and the most tedious; the most energizing and the most depleting; the most simple and the most complicated; the most admired and the most ridiculed; the most peaceful and the most frantic; the most appreciated and the most taken for granted; the most supernatural and the most mundane; the most Christian and the most unchristian.

Ministers who only experience the positive side of this life are either participating in a very select type of ministry or are repressing the realities that threaten them. Ministers who only experience the negative side of this life do so because they are saddled with unrealistic expectations, are overworking and underenjoying life, are working with too many difficult people or ministers, or are deficient in the competencies necessary to be reasonably successful in their work.

Ministry, when properly lived, is an almost daily mixture of both sides of life—positive and negative—a phenomenon that reflects the life of Jesus with reasonable accuracy.

To keep a balanced life—or better, a life whose positive and negative sides excite one another and enable the person to grow—ministers must be able to remain sufficiently close to God so that ministry is neither simply a stage upon which their narcissistic needs get met, creating an ongoing state of euphoria, nor just another grueling, low-paying job that causes a near constant state of depression.

Ministers must strive to get a sufficient number of needs met outside of ministry so that their ministry does not become their sole source of nourishment, causing either malnutrition because needs are not getting met in ministry, or causing ministers to feed on the very people they are supposed to be feeding.

Ministers should possess realistic expectations both of themselves and of others. This means that ministers may expect to be increasingly successful with a large number of people, but also realize that they will not be able to help a certain percentage of people. It also means that ministers may expect a fair number of people to be cooperative with them, but know that a certain percentage will be unable or unwilling to cooperate.

Finally, ministers need to keep both themselves and their ministry in a proper perspective. They should realize that although they are a part of God's plan, they are neither God nor responsible for all of God's plan. Ministers must be content to do their own modest—but important—part and allow God and others to take up the slack.

No minister can be all the right things to all of the people all of the time. But for each minister, this year can be a little better than last year, and next year a little better than this year. I hope this book can be of some help in this process.

"In the meantime . . . , we wish you happiness; try to grow perfect; help one another. Be united; live in peace, and the God of love and peace will be with you." (2 Cor. 13:11)

Endnotes

INTRODUCTION

1. United States Catholic Conference, *As One Who Serves: Reflections on the Pastoral Ministry of Priests in the United States* (Washington, D.C.: Publications Office, U.S. Catholic Conference, 1977), 19.
2. Oscar E. Feucht, *Everyone a Minister* (St. Louis: Concordia Publishing House, 1981), 37.

CHAPTER 1: THE PSYCHOLOGICALLY AND PASTORALLY EFFECTIVE MINISTER

1. United States Catholic Conference, *As One Who Serves: Reflections on the Pastoral Ministry of Priests in the United States* (Washington, D.C.: Publications Office, U.S. Catholic Conference, 1977), 55.

CHAPTER 3: HELPS AND HINDRANCES IN MINISTRY

1. Anthony Trollope, *Barchester Chronicles*, vol. 1 (New York: Dodd, Mead & Co., 1914), 64.
2. Henri J. M. Nouwen, *Creative Ministry* (Garden City, N.Y.: Doubleday & Co., 1978), 35.
3. William J. Bausch, *Traditions, Tensions, Transitions in Ministry* (Mystic, Conn.: Twenty-Third Publications, 1982), 13.
4. Richie Herink, ed., *The Psychotherapy Handbook* (New York: The New American Library, Inc., 1980), ii.
5. Charles E. Curran, *The Crisis in Priestly Ministry* (Notre Dame, Ind.: Fides Publishers, Inc., 1972), 33.
6. Annie Dillard, *Context*, vol. 16, no. 21 (December 1, 1984): 3. Writing to another author about self-worth and one's relationship to one's work, the poet Annie Dillard offers some advice that applies equally well to ministers: "Separate yourself from your work. A book you made isn't you any more than is a chair you made, or a soup. It's just something you made once. If you ever want to make another one, it, too, will be just another hat in the ring, another widow's mite, another broken offering which God has long understood is the best we humans can do—we're forgiven in advance. It doesn't much matter what we do. I comfort myself with this thought. You may not find it comforting, but I sure do."
7. Gerard Fourez, *A Sensible Guide to Prayer* (Chicago: Claretian Publications, 1975), 17–18.
8. Karl Rahner, *On Prayer* (New York: Paulist Press, 1958), 9.

CHAPTER 4: DEALING WITH SEXUAL ISSUES

1. Pope Paul VI, *Humanae Vitae* (Boston: Daughters of St. Paul, 1968), 22.
2. Morton Hunt, *Sexual Behavior in the 1970's* (New York: Playboy Press, 1974), 72–88.
3. Ibid., 74.
4. R. K. Greenbank, "Are Medical Students Learning Psychiatry?" *Pennsylvania Medical Journal* 64 (1961): 989–92.
5. Harold Lief and Arne Karlan, eds., *Sexual Education in Medicine* (New York: Spectrum, 1976), 28.
6. Hunt, *Sexual Behavior*, 75.
7. John H. Gagnon, William Simon, and Alan J. Berger, "Some Aspects of Sexual Adjustment in Early and Later Adolescence," in *The Psychology of Adolescence*, ed. Joseph Zubin and Alfred Freedman (New York: Grune and Stratton, 1970), 275–98.
8. William H. Masters, Virginia E. Johnson, and Robert C. Kolodny, *Human Sexuality*, 2nd ed. (Boston: Little, Brown & Co., 1985), 367.
9. Raymond Rosen and Linda Reich Rosen, *Human Sexuality* (New York: Alfred A. Knopf, 1981), 272.
10. Hunt, *Sexual Behavior*, 149.
11. M. Zelnick and J. F. Kantner, "The probability of premarital intercourse," *Social Science Research*, 1 (1972): 335–41.
12. Hunt, *Sexual Behavior*, 150.
13. U.S. Dept. of Commerce Bureau of the Census, 1982, in *Family Life Educator*, vol. 2, no. 1 (1983): 19.
14. Ibid.
15. C. Tavris and S. Sadd, *The Redbook Report on Female Sexuality* (New York: Delacorte Press, 1977), 34.
16. Rosen and Rosen, *Human Sexuality*, 272.
17. Hunt, *Sexual Behavior*, 150.
18. Aaron Hass, as quoted in Carole Wade Offir, *Human Sexuality* (New York: Harcourt Brace Jovanovich, Inc., 1982), 331.
19. Robert Sorensen, *Adolescent Sexuality in Contemporary America* (New York: World Publishing Co., 1973), as quoted in Bryan Strong and Rebecca Reynolds, *Understanding Our Sexuality* (St. Paul: West Publishing Co., 1982), 297.
20. Bryan Strong, et al., *Human Sexuality*, 2nd ed. (St. Paul: West Publishing Co., 1981), 29.
21. Offir, *Human Sexuality*, 324.
22. Elizabeth Rice Allgeier and Albert Richard Allgeier, *Sexual Interactions* (Lexington, Mass.: D.C. Heath and Co., 1984), 519–20.
23. Ibid., 525,
24. Sorenson, *Adolescent Sexuality*, as cited in Rosen and Rosen, *Human Sexuality*, 271.
25. Strong and Reynolds, *Understanding Our Sexuality*, 303–04.
26. Offir, *Human Sexuality*, 232.
27. Masters, Johnson, and Kolodny, *Human Sexuality*, 414,
28. Wardell B. Pomeroy, "Normal Vs. Abnormal Sex," *Sexology* 32 (1966): 436–39.
29. Charles H. McCaghy, "Child Molesting," *Sexual Behavior* 1 (1971): 16–24.
30. Allgeier and Allgeier, *Sexual Interactions*, 511.
31. Hunt, *Sexual Behavior*, 155.

32. Senate of Priests, Archdiocese of San Francisco, *Ministry and Homosexuality in the Archdiocese of San Francisco* (1983), 38.
33. Richard McCormick, "Notes on Moral Theology," *Theological Studies* 34 (1973): 90.
34. *Declaration on Certain Questions Regarding Sexual Ethics* (Rome: Sacred Congregation for the Doctrine of the Faith, 1976), as quoted in Anthony Kosnick et. al., *Human Sexuality: New Directions in American Catholic Thought* (New York: Paulist Press, 1977), 308.
35. Ibid, 306.
36. Thomas Aquinas, *Summa Theologica*, I–II, q. 94, art. 4.
37. As used in this context, the term "morally responsible decision" means that an individual *responded* to the moral issues involved to the best of his or her ability at a particular time.
38. Daniel C. McGuire, "The Vatican on Sex," *Commonweal*, vol. 103, no. 5 (February 27, 1976): 138.
39. Andre Guindon, *The Sexual Language* (Ottawa: University of Ottawa Press, 1976), 288.

CHAPTER 5: THE PERSONALLY REFLECTIVE MINISTER

1. James C. Fenhagen, *Mutual Ministry* (New York: The Seabury Press, 1977), 25.
2. Andrew M. Greeley, "Priest, Church, and the Future from a Sociological Viewpoint," in *Future Forms of Ministry*, ed. Richard A. McCormick and George J. Dyer (Chicago: National Federation of Priests' Councils in conjunction with *Chicago Studies*, 1971), 14.
3. William E. Hulme, *Your Pastor's Problems* (Minneapolis: Augsburg Publishing House, 1977), 25.
4. Fred Brown, *Faith Without Religion* (New York: SCM Press, Ltd., 1971), 94.
5. Urban T. Holmes III, *Spirituality for Ministry* (New York: Harper & Row, 1982), 44.
6. Ernest Marvin, "Ministry in Ferment," in *Ministry in Question*, ed. Alec Gilmore (London: Darton, Longman & Todd, Ltd., 1971), 65.
7. Seward Hiltner, *Ferment in the Ministry* (Nashville: Abingdon Press, 1969), 22.
8. United States Catholic Conference, *As One Who Serves: Reflections on the Pastoral Ministry of Priests in the United States* (Washington, D.C.: Publications Office, U.S. Catholic Conference, 1977), 56.
9. Gerd Theissen, *A Critical Faith* (Philadelphia: Fortress Press, 1979), 19.
10. Fenhagen, *Mutual Ministry*, 25.
11. James D. Whitehead and Evelyn Eaton Whitehead, *Method in Ministry* (New York: The Seabury Press, 1981), 156–57.
12. Holmes, *Spirituality for Ministry*, 48.
13. Bernard Basset, *And Would You Believe It!* (New York: Doubleday & Co., 1976), 27.
14. Andrew M. Greeley, *Uncertain Trumpet* (New York: Sheed & Ward, 1968), 29.
15. Henri J. M. Nouwen, *The Wounded Healer* (Garden City, N.Y.: Doubleday & Co., 1972), 44.
16. Tad Guzie, *The Book of Sacramental Basics* (Ramsey, N.J.: Paulist Press, 1981), 73.

17. William J. O'Malley, *The Roots of Unbelief* (New York: Paulist Press, 1976), 42–43.
18. Urban T. Holmes III, *The Priest in Community* (New York: The Seabury Press, 1978), 125.
19. Bernard Haring, *Faith and Morality in the Secular Age* (New York: Doubleday & Co., 1973), 99.
20. Eugene C. Kennedy, *Believing* (Garden City, N.Y.: Doubleday & Co., 1977), 50.
21. David W. Augsburger, *Anger and Assertiveness in Pastoral Care* (Philadelphia: Fortress Press, 1979), viii.
22. Karl Barth, "The Gift of Freedom: Foundation of Evangelical Ethics," as cited by Charles B. Ketcham and James F. Day, eds., *Faith and Freedom/Essays in Contemporary Theology* (New York: Weybright and Talley, 1969), 77.
23. James E. Dittes, *Minister on the Spot* (Princeton, N.J.: Pilgrim Press, 1970), 34.
24. Hartzell Spence, *The Clergy and What They Do* (New York: Franklin Watts, Inc., 1961), 47.
25. Henri J. M. Nouwen, *The Living Reminder* (New York: The Seabury Press, 1981), 12.
26. James Tunstead Burtchaell, *Philemon's Problem: The Daily Dilemma of the Christian* (Chicago: Foundation for Adult Catechetical Teaching Aids, 1973), 47.
27. Spence, *The Clergy and What They Do*, 22.
28. David P. O'Neill, *The Priest in Crisis: A Study in Role Change* (Dayton, Ohio: Pflaum Press, 1968), 212.
29. Hans Kung, *Freedom Today* (New York: Sheed & Ward, 1966), 57.
30. Andrew M. Greeley et. al., *Parish, Priest, and People* (Chicago: Thomas More Press, 1981), 203.
31. Joseph J. Blomjous, *Priesthood in Crisis* (Milwaukee: Bruce Publishing Co., 1969), 92–93.
32. Greeley, *Uncertain Trumpet*, 62.
33. Dermot A. Lane, *The Reality of Jesus* (New York: Paulist Press, 1975), 33.

Bibliography

*Augsburger, David W. *Anger and Assertiveness in Pastoral Care.* Philadelphia: Fortress Press, 1979.

Basset, Bernard. *And Would You Believe It!* New York: Doubleday & Company, 1976.

*Bausch, William J., *Traditions, Tensions, Transitions in Ministry.* Mystic, Conn.: Twenty-Third Publications, 1982.

Blomjous, Joseph J. *Priesthood in Crisis.* Milwaukee: Bruce Publishing Co., 1969.

Brown, Fred. *Faith Without Religion.* New York: SCM Press, Ltd., 1971.

*Brown, Raymond E. *Biblical Reflections on Crises in the Church.* New York: Paulist Press, 1975.

*Burtchaell, James Tunstead. *Philemon's Problem: The Daily Dilemma of the Christian.* Chicago: Foundation for Adult Catechetical Teaching Aids, 1973.

Callahan, Daniel. *Honesty in the Church.* New York: Charles Scribner's Sons, 1965.

*Cavanagh, Michael E. *The Counseling Experience: A Theoretical and Practical Approach.* Monterey: Brooks/Cole Publishing Co., 1982.

*Cavanagh, Michael E. *Make Your Tomorrow Better: A Psychological Guide for Singles, Parents, and the Entire Family.* New York: Paulist Press, 1980.

Cavanagh, Michael E. *What To Do When You're Feeling Guilty.* Chicago: Claretian Publications, 1978.

*Cavanagh, Michael E. "The Impact of Psychosexual Growth on Marriage and Religious Life." *Human Development* vol. 4 (Fall 1983): 16–24.

*Cavanagh, Michael E. "Psychotherapeutic Issues in Religious Life." *Human Development* vol. 3 (Summer 1982): 24–30.

*Cooke, Bernard. *Rethinking Your Faith.* Chicago: Claretian Publications, 1972.

*Coridan, James, ed. *Sexism and Church Law.* New York: Paulist Press, 1977.

Curran, Charles E. *The Crisis in Priestly Ministry.* Notre Dame, Ind.: Fides Publishers, Inc., 1972.

Dedek, John F. *Contemporary Sexual Morality.* New York: Sheed & Ward, 1971.

Edwards, Paul. *The Theology of Priesthood.* Hales Corners, Wis.: Clergy Book Service, 1974.

Egan, Gerard. *The Skilled Helper.* Monterey: Brooks/Cole Publishing Co., 1982.

Faricy, Robert. *Praying for Inner Healing.* New York: Paulist Press, 1979.

Fenhagen, James C. *Mutual Ministry.* New York: The Seabury Press, 1977.

*Feucht, Oscar E. *Everyone a Minister.* St. Louis: Concordia Publishing House, 1981.

*Goergen, Donald. *The Sexual Celibate.* New York: The Seabury Press, 1974.

Greeley, Andrew M. *Uncertain Trumpet.* New York: Sheed & Ward, 1968.

*Greeley, Andrew M., Mary Durkin, John Shea, David Tracy, and William McCready. *Parish, Priest, and People.* Chicago: Thomas More Press, 1981.

Greenbank, R. K. "Are Medical Students Learning Psychiatry?" *Pennsylvania Medical Journal* 64 (1961): 989–92.

*Groome, Thomas H. *Christian Religious Education.* San Francisco: Harper & Row, 1980.

Guzie, Tad. *The Book of Sacramental Basics.* Ramsey, N.J.: Paulist Press, 1981.

*Hanigan, James P. *What Are They Saying About Sexual Morality?* New York: Paulist Press, 1982.

Haring, Bernard. *Faith and Morality in the Secular Age.* New York: Doubleday & Co., 1973.

Hiltner, Seward. *Ferment in the Ministry.* New York: Abingdon Press, 1969.

Holmes, Urban T., III. *The Future Shape of Ministry.* New York: The Seabury Press, 1971.

*Holmes, Urban T., III. *The Priest in Community.* New York: The Seabury Press, 1978.

Holmes, Urban T., III. *Spirituality for Ministry.* New York: Harper & Row, 1982.

Hooker, E. "The adjustment of the male overt homosexual." *Journal of Projective Techniques* 22 (1957): 33–54.

Hunt, Morton. *Sexual Behavior in the 1970's.* New York: Playboy Press, 1974.

*Keane, Philip. *Sexual Morality: A Catholic Perspective.* New York: Paulist Press, 1977.

*Kelsey, Morton T. *Prophetic Ministry.* New York: Crossroad, 1982.

Kennedy, Eugene C. *Believing.* Garden City, N.Y.: Doubleday & Co., 1977.

*Kennedy, Eugene C. *Sexual Counseling: A Practical Guide for Non-Professional Counselors.* New York: Continuum, 1977.

Ketcham, Charles B., and James F. Day, eds. *Faith and Freedom/Essays in Contemporary Theology.* New York: Weybright & Talley, 1969.

Kirvan, John J. *The Restless Believers.* New York: Paulist Press, 1966.

*Kosnik, Anthony, et al. *Human Sexuality: New Directions in American Catholic Thought.* New York: Paulist Press, 1977.

Kung, Hans. *Freedom Today.* New York: Sheed & Ward, 1966.

*Kung, Hans. *On Being a Christian.* Translated by Edward Quinn. New York: Simon & Schuster, 1978.

Kung, Hans. *Truthfulness: The Future of the Church.* New York: Sheed & Ward, 1968.

*Lane, Dermot A. *The Reality of Jesus.* New York: Paulist Press, 1975.

Lewis, C. S. *Mere Christianity.* New York: Macmillan Co., 1960.

Lief, Harold, and Arne Karlan, eds. *Sexual Education in Medicine.* New York: Spectrum, 1976.

Maloney, George A. *Inward Stillness.* Denville, N.J.: Dimension Books, 1976.

Martin, David G. *Counseling and Therapy Skills.* Monterey: Brooks/Cole Publishing Co., 1983.

Martin, Ralph P. *Worship in the Early Church.* Grand Rapids: William B. Eerdmans Publishing Co., 1964.

Marty, Martin E. *Varieties of Unbelief.* Garden City, N.Y.: Doubleday Anchor Books, 1966.

Masters, William H., Virginia E. Johnson, and Robert C. Kolodny. *Human Sexuality.* Boston: Little, Brown & Co., 1982.

*Nelson, James B. *Embodiment: An Approach to Sexuality and Christian Theology.* Minneapolis: Augsburg Publishing House, 1978.

*Nouwen, Henri J. M. *Creative Ministry.* Garden City, N.Y.: Doubleday & Co., 1978.

Nouwen, Henri J. M. *Reaching Out.* Garden City, N.Y.: Doubleday & Co., 1975.

*Nouwen, Henri J. M. *The Way of the Heart.* New York: The Seabury Press, 1981.

*Nouwen, Henri J. M. *The Wounded Healer.* Garden City, N.Y.: Doubleday & Co., 1972.

Offir, Carole Wade. *Human Sexuality.* New York: Harcourt Brace Jovanovich, Inc., 1982.

*Ohanneson, Joan. *And They Felt No Shame.* Minneapolis: Winston Press, 1983.

O'Malley, William J. *The Roots of Unbelief.* New York: Paulist Press, 1976.

*O'Meara, Thomas Franklin. *Theology of Ministry.* New York: Paulist Press, 1983.

O'Neill, David P. *The Priest in Crisis: A Study in Role Change.* Dayton, Ohio: Pflaum Press, 1968.

Peplau, L. A., Z. Rubin, and C. T. Hill. "Sexual intimacy in dating relationships." *Journal of Social Issues* 33, no. 2 (1977): 86–109.

*Perkins, Pheme. *Ministering in the Pauline Churches*. New York: Paulist Press, 1982.

*Powell, John. *A Reason to Live! A Reason to Die*. Niles, Ill.: Argus Communications, 1975.

*Provost, James H. *Official Ministry in a New Age*. Washington, D.C.: Canon Law Society of America, 1981.

Rademacher, William J. *The Practical Guide for Parish Councils*. Mystic, Conn.: Twenth-Third Publications, 1979.

Rahner, Karl. *The Christian Commitment*. New York: Sheed & Ward, 1963.

Rahner, Karl. *Concern for the Church*. New York: Crossroad, 1981.

Rahner, Karl. *On Prayer*. New York: Paulist Press, 1958.

Rosen, Raymond, and Linda Reich Rosen. *Human Sexuality*. New York: Alfred A. Knopf, 1981.

Sanford, John A. *The Kingdom Within*. Philadelphia: J. B. Lippincott Co., 1970.

*Sanford, John A. *Ministry Burnout*. New York: Paulist Press, 1982.

Schaller, Lyle E. *Parish Planning*. Nashville: Abingdon Press, 1971.

Schillebeeckx, Edward. *Ministry: Leadership in the Community of Jesus Christ*. New York: Crossroad, 1981.

*Senior, Donald. *Jesus*. Dayton, Ohio: Pflaum Press, 1975.

Smith, S. "Teenagers and sex: Knowledge still lacking." *Los Angeles Times*, January 27, 1980.

Sorensen, Robert. *Adolescent Sexuality in Contemporary America*. New York: World Publishing Co., 1973.

Spence, Hartzell. *The Clergy and What They Do*. New York: Franklin Watts, Inc., 1961.

Strong, Bryan, Sam Wilson, Mina Robbins, and Thomas Johns. *Human Sexuality*, 2nd ed. St. Paul: West Publishing Co., 1981.

*Strong, Bryan, and Rebecca Reynolds. *Understanding Our Sexuality*. St. Paul: West Publishing Co., 1982.

Tavris, C., and S. Sadd. *The Redbook Report on Female Sexuality*. New York: Delacorte Press, 1977,

Taylor, Michael J. *Sex: Thoughts for Contemporary Christians*. Garden City, N.Y.: Doubleday & Co., 1972.

*Theissen, Gerd. *A Critical Faith*. Philadelphia: Fortress Press, 1979.

Tillich, Paul. *Dynamics of Faith*. New York: Harper Colophon Books, 1957.

Van Kaam, Adrian, and Susan Muto. *Am I Living a Spiritual Life?* Denville, N.J.: Dimension Books, 1978.

Victor, Jeffrey S. *Human Sexuality: A Social Psychological Approach*. New York: Prentice Hall, 1980.

*Whitehead, James D., and Evelyn Eaton Whitehead. *Method in Ministry*. New York: The Seabury Press, 1981.

Zelnick, M., and J. F. Kantner. "The probability of premarital intercourse." *Social Science Research* 1 (1972): 335–41.

As One Who Serves: Reflections on the Pastoral Ministry of Priests in the United States. Washington, D.C.: Publications Office, United States Catholic Conference, 1977.

"Gallup Poll Survey: Americans' Attitudes Toward Gays." *Family Life Educator* 2, no. 1 (Fall 1983): 21.

Homosexuality and Social Justice. Report of the Task Force on Gay/Lesbian Issues, July 1982, San Francisco Commission on Social Justice, 1982.

Sharing the Light of Faith: National Catechetical Directory for Catholics of the United States. Washington, D.C.: United States Catholic Conference, Department of Education, 1979.

The references preceded by an asterisk are especially recommended as books that most ministers would find particularly helpful.